SIGNPOSTS FOR THE JOURNEY

VOLUME ONE: REFLECTIONS OF A SERVANT LEADER ON MOSES, MINISTRY, MONEY AND MORE

SIGNPOSTS FOR THE JOURNEY

VOLUME I
REFLECTIONS OF A SERVANT LEADER ON MOSES, MINISTRY, MONEY, AND MORE…

BY JON BYLER

LEADERSSERVE

WWW.LEADERSSERVE.COM

SIGNPOSTS FOR THE JOURNEY

VOLUME I

by Jon Byler

Copyright © 2015 Global Disciples

ISBN-10: 0-9770085-3-3

ISBN-13: 978-0-9770085-3-7

Unless otherwise noted, Scripture quotations are taken from the HOLY BIBLE, NEW INTERNATIONAL VERSION, Copyright © 1973, 1978, 1984 International Bible Society. Used by permission of Zondervan Bible Publishers.

Published by LeadersServe

www.LeadersServe.com

The cover design, interior art, and painting, Sycamore Path, by Rachel Byler © TheColorfulCatStudio 2013

DEDICATION

This book is dedicated to my heroes, pastors, and church leaders in the developing world who are courageously forging ahead with a totally new pattern of leadership. Their courage to follow Jesus' example, even when it clashes with their culture, is an inspiration to me. Your stories of faithfulness bring strength to my soul, and I would gladly wash your feet to encourage you on the journey. May these chapters give you strength and hope for your journey and be signposts pointing you more and more to the example of Jesus.

CONTENTS

INTRODUCTION

I'm passionate about leadership and have devoted my life to be the best leader I can be and develop others in every way possible. Learning to lead like Jesus is a lifelong journey of growing in understanding what His model of leadership means for my life situations. Even after 20 years of focus on this subject, I'm continually learning more as I reflect on what scripture teaches, as I observe other leaders around me and as I read what others have written.

Each of us is on a similar journey. Some of you have been leading much longer than I; others are just beginning. Some are involved in church leadership; others serve in business or their profession. All of us have areas of influence which God has entrusted uniquely to us. Growing as a leader is simply being a faithful steward of the influence He has, in His grace, allowed us to exercise. As we grow on the journey, we bring greater glory to Him and more fully accomplish all that He intends for us to be and do.

Think of this book as signposts on the journey. Signposts reveal the way forward often with choices which lead to different destinations. Our leadership journey is likewise filled with daily choices of how we will exercise our influence. Each decision can take us in the direction of becoming a servant leader more like Jesus or a selfish leader following our own way. It is easy to choose the path that feels most natural to us or which we have seen others model. It takes courage to choose the path of servant leadership.

Each of the signposts in this book provides encouragement to make the choices that move us in the direction of servant leadership. Each chapter touches on a specific area of leadership and calls us to learn more about how to lead as servants, like Jesus.

Walk slowly on this journey, reflecting thoughtfully on what the signposts reveal. Take several days or a week with each chapter, reading it several times and spending some time to write out answers to the reflection questions for personal application. Take more time with those that call for more action on your part. If you are able to go through this journey with a group, it can be an even more powerful experience as you share together and hold each other accountable to continued growth.

These reflections were originally distributed as bi-weekly e-zines, *Reflections for Servant Leaders,* and are now published in book and electronic format. I acknowledge with gratitude the hard work of Samantha Petersheim and Linda Boll who spent hours preparing this volume for publication. I also thank Rachel Byler, my daughter in law, for her creative work on the cover design.

Enjoy the signposts in this volume as you reflect on what it means to be bold yet humble; learn from the life and leadership of Moses, discover the quality checklist used by Paul and think about what servant leadership looks like at home.

Yours on the journey,

Jon Byler
2015

1. WHIPS AND WASHBASINS

Jesus, the greatest leader the world has ever known, picked up whips and drove the moneychangers out of the temple. *Jesus entered the temple area and drove out all who were buying and selling there. He overturned the tables of the money changers and the benches of those selling doves. "It is written," he said to them, "'My house will be called a house of prayer,' but you are making it a 'den of robbers'"* (Matthew 21:12-13). Later He sat down with His disciples and took a towel and washbasin to show them a picture of servant leadership. *After that, he poured water into a basin and began to wash his disciples' feet, drying them with the towel that was wrapped around him (John 13:5).* How could the hands of Jesus wield a whip and then humbly wash feet?

This is a paradox with which all who seek to lead like Jesus must wrestle. On one hand, Christian leaders hear voices calling for "servant" leadership, which often implies passive leadership by consensus. Other voices cry urgently for action and "bold" leadership. What are we to do with the conflicting voices and the example of Jesus? What does it really mean to be a servant leader?

Servant leaders lead with strength. Jesus' action with the whip looks radical, extreme, and the opposite of everything we associate with servant leadership. We wrongly assume that servant leaders are not strong leaders and therefore any display of strength is wrong. This thinking produces weak leaders who are afraid to use their God-given authority. But Jesus cannot be called a weak leader and in this act, He demonstrated bold, courageous leadership. Jesus was not content to allow what God intended for good to be abused by men. He would not stand by without acting. Servant leaders are also called to change their world with strong, effective leadership. Our homes, our churches, our business or professions need strong leadership. Wrongs need to be made right and we are called to lead with strength.

Servant leaders have a heart of service. Behind the whip, what was in the heart of Jesus? He was not on a self-righteous rampage. He had no selfish agenda. He was not looking for publicity or trying to make a name for himself. Rather, He was boldly confronting an obvious wrong and using His authority to serve others, not Himself. His act must be understood in light of His heart and He clearly had a heart to serve. As He stooped to wash the feet of His disciples, He revealed that His heart was that of a servant leader. The motive of a servant leader is very different, even when outward actions look similar to what other leaders are doing. They are called to serve with the humility of Jesus.

Servant leaders balance strength and service. Jesus perfectly balanced strong, bold action with the heart of a servant. In doing so, He defines servant leadership as both leadership and service. One without the other will not be adequate. Some leaders are powerful and act, but their hearts are not humble. Others have the heart of a servant but don't act! The example of Jesus calls for both. Servant leaders are called to lead! They should be bold and courageous. At the same time their heart focus is on the needs of others instead of their own needs. They readily acknowledge that their tendency is to use a whip when their own agenda has been attacked, when their own insecurities have been exposed, or when they want to demonstrate authority. They realize that in these situations the focus is on self, not others, and their leadership is selfish, not servant leadership. A whip without the heart of a servant will only leave bruises on those it drives out. But in the hands of a servant the whip can bring Godly change.

Sorting out motives with a heart that is desperately wicked is no easy task. But Jesus was fully human and knows our weaknesses. Still He calls us to follow His example of leading with the heart of a servant…even when it means picking up the whip. The whip is an *act* of leadership; the basin reflects the *heart* of leadership. In the next chapters we'll look more closely at this theme as we consider what it means to have bold humility.

For further reflection and discussion:

1. In what ways have I confused strong leadership and servant leadership?

2. Is it more natural for me to lead with boldness or to serve?

   What is the result?

3. Do I allow other's expectations of leadership to shape my obedience to the example of Jesus?

4. What other biblical examples can you think of where leaders used 'whips'?

Was the result positive or negative?

2. PROFILES IN BOLD HUMILITY: JESUS

One time Jesus boldly picked up a whip and drove the money changers out of the temple. Then, on another occasion, He humbly washed the feet of His disciples. So what are we to do, wash feet or use a whip? Jesus' example calls us to balance both of them in what I will refer to as "bold humility." In this chapter, I will continue to look at the life of Jesus as He demonstrates bold humility. In the following chapters, we'll examine other biblical profiles that demonstrate bold humility.

The word "servant" too often is misunderstood to mean weakness and lack of assertiveness. Servants are expected to do what others want. Leaders who understand service in this way genuinely love others, have a heart of gold, and are ready to do whatever is asked. But they don't have the courage required to lead with boldness and not much happens as a result. This may be service, but it is not leadership!

Other leaders succeed in being bold as lions. Nothing stops them. They are courageous world changers, filled with vision and action. But no one would describe them as humble!

The power of Jesus' leadership came in the way He combined these two elements. No one dare accuse Jesus of being a weak leader. Yet, His humility is just as evident. His actions were strong; His heart was tender. His examples of chasing out the moneychangers (John 2) and washing the feet of the disciples (John 13) help us understand two principles of servant leadership.

Boldness requires a servant leader to demonstrate passionate power. When Jesus observed what was happening in the temple, He was justifiably upset. What was happening was an affront to God's plan and purpose for His people. He was consumed with zeal for His Father's house and it led to bold action. His passionate boldness came from His conviction that He was called by God to make a difference in His world. It took tremendous courage for Jesus to confront the existing powers in place at the temple. He demonstrated passion for a cause that every servant leader should imitate. The world desperately needs leaders who have the courage and passion to confront wrong and make it right. You can be a servant without passion, but you cannot be a leader without courage.

Humility enables a servant leader to demonstrate release of power. The account of Jesus washing the feet of His disciples demonstrates a willing release of power. Jesus took off His outer robe and in doing so laid aside all privilege and power which He had as the leader of the group. He stooped to do the literal work of a servant as he cleaned their dirty feet. His humility came from the recognition that God's call on His life was not about Himself, it was for the purposes of the Father. All servant leaders are called to lay down their rights and privileges for God's purposes. They recognize the power given to them is not their own or for themselves, so they can lay it down and perform the lowest of tasks.

Many leaders struggle to find a balance between

being bold and humble. Jesus models the way as He led with astounding boldness and amazing humility. He was comfortable exercising power and authority and at ease to lay it down. May we become more like Him in our leadership at home, in our work, and in our church!

For further reflection and discussion:

1. What is the most courageous action I have taken in my leadership?

2. From what motivation did this action come? Was it focused on my own ambitions or God's glory?

3. How does my calling from God provide courage to act?

4. Is there something in my leadership about which I have a powerful passion?

    If so, how do I express it? If not, what is the result of this lack?

5. When have I recently released power or stepped back from assertive leadership?

    Was this easy or difficult for me?

6. As I reflect on my leadership, am I most often bold or humble? What is the result of this on those I lead?

7. What steps do I need to take to bring a healthy balance to these two areas?

3. PROFILES IN BOLD HUMILITY: JOSEPH

What should servant leaders be, bold or humble? We are called to both as we already observed from Jesus who used whips and washbasins in His leadership. In this chapter, we will reflect on the life of Joseph who also demonstrated a balance between boldness and humility, especially in the area of planning. Joseph, the son of Jacob, lived a privileged life as a young boy and clearly had a dream for a significant future. But after his brothers sold him into slavery, his plans seemed to be crushed until 13 years later when he rose to become the prime minister of Egypt. In that position he led the country through 14 years of economic upheaval that makes any current leadership challenges seem mild! What can we learn from Joseph about bold humility in the area of planning?

Boldness requires a servant leader to strategically dream and plan. As a 17 year old, Joseph had a plan for his life. He boldly shared his vision of leadership with his family. He was out to change the world and expected everyone around him to bow down! His dream was so bold that his father, who loved Joseph as a favorite son, rebuked him. Joseph's brothers, like so many today, didn't have a dream and reacted negatively to Joseph's visionary plan.

For 13 years of slavery and imprisonment, Joseph's plans seemed to be crushed. But he worked hard and slowly developed the character and skills needed to accomplish his plan. He learned to lead in Potiphar's household and then in prison. In prison, he learned how to listen to the dreams of others. After interpreting the dream of Pharaoh, Joseph shared with the ruler a comprehensive plan to deal with the pending crisis. It was bold and ambitious; it was clear and concrete. His plan provided details on personnel needed, production goals, warehouse management, record-keeping and distribution networks! Pharaoh quickly recognized that he was listening to a bold, visionary, strategic planner and rightly appointed him to oversee the country.

Servant leaders are not afraid to dream and plan strategically. They boldly look beyond the present into the future and see possibilities where others only see problems. They dream of a world in which lives are transformed and see their church or their business as a part of that plan. They are willing to stand and declare as Joseph did, "I have a dream."

Humility enables a servant leader to acknowledge God's plan. As a 17 year old, Joseph was bold but not yet humble. His dream was about people bowing down to him, not how he would serve them. He correctly saw that he would be in a position of leadership but didn't yet understand how leaders serve those they lead. By the time he was the prime minister of Egypt he could humbly recognize that God's plans were far bigger than his own and that what he earlier saw as his dreams were really God's dreams. God wanted to use Joseph to save his own family and to bring them to Egypt for what would be the next 400 years of God's story. Joseph worked hard, but at this point was able to say to Pharaoh, *"I cannot do it, but*

God will give Pharaoh the answer he desires" (Genesis 41:16). He was able to humbly acknowledge to his brothers that the things they intended for harm were used of God to accomplish the plan.

Servant leaders recognize that God calls them to bold, strategic planning, but balanced with deep humility. They must, and will work hard, but acknowledge that it will take more than human effort and planning to accomplish God's purposes. Their lives demonstrate Proverbs 16:9, *In his heart a man plans his course, but the LORD determines his steps.*

For further reflection and discussion:

1. Consider the following passages from Joseph's story. In what ways do these passages illustrate Joseph's ability to plan boldly or his humility as he carries out the plan? (Gen. 37:2-28; 39:1-6, 20-23; 40:1-23; 41:14-37; 45:4-8; 47:13-27; 50:15-21)

2. When it comes to planning, do you most naturally lead with boldness or humility?

    Identify a recent example of how this was evident. When you follow your natural tendency towards boldness or humility, what is the outcome?

3. What needs to change for you to be more balanced?

4. What is your dream? Is it big enough to require God's help to accomplish?

    Is it focused on your own goals or God's purposes for your life?

5. Have you allowed the responses of others to keep you from moving forward with boldness in strategic planning?

6. In what ways do you walk in humility as you plan strategically?

7. Have you recognized how God's plans are bigger than yours and how He will use yours to accomplish His?

8. When you work hard, do you acknowledge that your success depends not on your own effort but His blessing?

4. PROFILES IN BOLD HUMILITY: MOSES

Humility is often seen as a sign of weakness. But Moses is an example of a servant leader who demonstrates that humility can be bold. He is described as *"more humble than anyone else on the face of the earth"* (Numbers 12:3). At the same time he was a bold and courageous leader who fought for his people. What do these two characteristics look like in the life of a servant leader?

Boldness requires a servant leader to fight for the people. Moses fought, both figuratively and literally, for the freedom of his people. He boldly marched into Pharaoh's court and repeated God's words, "Let my people go!" This was not a timid, cowardly approach. He did not check the opinion polls before moving forward. Moses was a bold, servant leader who found a cause worthy of a struggle and stepped up to the task of leading a revolution. He did not initially consider himself adequate for the task and resisted God's call, but ultimately realized that it was not about his ability but God's agenda for His people. Then Moses became the bold visionary leader who led a nation to freedom.

Many leaders fight for themselves and to exercise their own authority. They win battles and achieve goals for themselves. Other leaders hold positions of influence but lack the vision and courage to call for action. They don't fight for anything. Servant leaders fight boldly, not for their own agenda, but to see God's purposes accomplished through those they lead. They view their family, business, work team, or congregation as the group that God has given them and they are not timid about expressing God's direction for this group. They are bold when they lead the charge against all opposition. They are courageous warriors, never content with the way things are! The boldness of servant leaders comes because they are fighting, not for themselves, but for others.

Humility enables a servant leader to intercede for the people. Moses, as a young man, had demonstrated an ability to be bold when he killed the Egyptian. But his boldness was not, at that point, tempered with humility. He needed another 40 years of leadership training before he was ready to serve with humility! At this point, Moses' leadership was characterized by continual conversation with God. God spoke to him; then Moses acted. He developed intimacy with God through continued conversation with Him. He became a leader with the humility to balance bold leadership with humble intercession. Nowhere was this demonstrated more clearly than when God was ready to destroy the nation for their rebellion at Horeb. Moses laid face-down for 40 days, crying out to God on behalf of the people. (Read the summary in Deuteronomy 9, a great chapter on servant leadership.) He was still fighting for the people, but this time the fight was not bold confrontation, but humble intercession.

When his own sister challenged his calling to leadership, Moses' responded with prayer for her healing.

That's a sign of humility! Servant leaders learn to humbly fight battles on their knees as they pray by name for those under their leadership. This humility keeps them balanced and provides a safeguard against fighting their own battles. When they rise up from their knees, they know when and how to be bold. As they exercise bold leadership they return to their knees to again hear from God. Servant leaders have learned not to fight for anything until they kneel over everything.

Then, and only then, they lead with bold humility.

For further reflection and discussion:

1. Read Numbers 12, the account of Moses and Miriam. How do I respond when someone challenges my authority as a leader?

2. What can I learn from Moses' response to this challenge?

3. What is most typical in my leadership, bold fighting or humble intercession? (If you are not sure, ask someone who follows you!)

4. In what ways does this imbalance reveal itself in my leadership?

5. In what ways have I demonstrated boldness in my leadership recently, "fighting" for my people?

6. What demonstrates that this fighting is not for my own purposes, but for God's design?

7. Are there ways in which I have been timid about expressing God's plan for those I lead? What do I need to change?

8. How do I pray regularly, by name, for those whom God has entrusted to my leadership?

   Do they know it?

9. In what way is God inviting me to strengthen this aspect of my leadership?

5. PROFILES IN BOLD HUMILITY: ESTHER

Esther has all the qualities of a movie heroine. She was the beautiful first lady in the empire of King Xerxes, a position filled with glamor and prestige. Her rise from an orphan in exile to this position of power has captivated readers for centuries. But behind the amazing story of her life is a powerful lesson in servant leadership. Esther boldly used her position to change the destiny of her people but did so with deep humility. What does she teach us today about servant leadership?

Boldness requires a servant leader to recognize and seize opportunity. Esther enjoyed her leadership position as the queen for at least four years before Haman, the enemy of the Jews, proposed his plot to destroy the Israelites. I imagine that she enjoyed the official duties of a queen and carried them out well. She, like many leaders today, was busy filling a role but not having much impact. She could have concluded that leadership was fun. But this crisis with Haman brought Queen Esther to the sudden realization that her position of leadership was not about herself but something far greater. Suddenly, her people faced a life and death situation and needed more than beautiful leadership, they needed bold leadership. Mordecai helped Esther recognize that she was in her royal position *"for such a time as this"* (Esther 4:14). Esther recognized that this was her moment and she, after calling for prayer, seized the opportunity boldly. She courageously went into the king's presence at the risk of her own life, not knowing as we do the outcome of her action. She courageously invited the king and Haman to one banquet and then another, where she shared with him the petition for her people. She boldly petitioned the king to overrule his decree through Haman. Then, after the revised decree was implemented, she boldly asked for more! At this point, her bold leadership saved her nation and established a new national holiday.

Servant leaders see their leadership positions as places given to them to see and seize opportunities God has provided. They are willing to boldly take risks, not for themselves, but for the good of those they serve. They recognize that leadership is about much more than privilege and public appearances. They understand they are leading *"for such a time as this."*

Humility enables a servant leader to seek God's favor. Esther's boldness did not come from reading leadership books or attending a workshop on self-esteem but from humbly seeking God. When first confronted with the crisis, she called for three days of prayer and fasting, for herself and her nation. This deliberate seeking of God's favor before acting gave Esther the boldness she needed to lead. It also emptied her of self and wrong motives. It enabled her to see God's perspective on her leadership and to approach the king with the perspective, *"if I perish, I perish"* (Esther 4:16). She now understood clearly that leadership was not about what she would get out of it. Her responsibility was to humbly obey. This humility continues through her story as she boldly exerts influence, but never dominates or draws attention to her role. She humbly resisted the temptation to move quickly, but waited on God's timing to share her request with the king. If she would have talked to the king the night of the first banquet, the gallows would not have been prepared for Mordecai. Neither would the king have read the record books during his sleepless night which resulted in honoring Mordecai. She humbly brings Mordecai into the palace when he is needed. Her boldness was always combined with a deep humility from seeking God's favor.

Boldness that comes from prayer and seeking God's favor is a powerful force of change. Servant leaders humbly seek God's favor, and then rise up with extraordinary boldness and selfless acts of courage. May it happen in your leadership and in mine!

For further reflection and discussion:

1. Take some time to read this story of Esther looking carefully at how she balanced boldness and humility. Make a list of examples of each trait as you read. What strikes you as significant?

2. What opportunities has God put before you which require bold leadership?

   What are the risks involved?

3. Does your leadership style naturally embrace risks quickly or are you more cautious by nature?

   What is the result?

4. Do you regularly find ways to seek God's favor?

5. Are there leadership issues in your experience right now which are significant enough to call for a day or three days of prayer and fasting?

6. Are there others whom you should call to join you in seeking God's favor?

6. PROFILES IN BOLD HUMILITY: DANIEL AND FRIENDS

Not many of us live and work in the presence of the president or top leader in our nation. In this environment, the pressure to conform is enormous and it takes tremendous boldness to take a stand. But, Daniel and his three friends demonstrate that boldness with humility is possible at these levels even when the official is a king with absolute power. What can we learn from Daniel, Shadrach, Meshach, and Abednego about how servant leaders combine boldness with humility?

Boldness requires a servant leader to take a stand for right. Daniel and his three friends faced huge moral challenges in life or death situations. Daniel, as a part of his three year orientation training, was tempted to compromise his convictions concerning diet. His three friends, in a huge public gathering, were commanded to bow down and worship an idol made by the king. In both situations, these leaders faced enormous peer pressure as everyone around them followed the instructions of the king. In both situations, disobedience to the king's commands could have cost them their lives. In such situations we can quickly rationalize reasons not to take a stand. We might think, "I'll bow my knee, but in my heart I'll worship God." Or, "It would be better to eat than to create a disturbance." Daniel and his friends showed enormous courage and boldly took a stand for what was right. *But Daniel resolved not to defile himself with the royal food and wine* (Daniel 1:8). The three men, when called into the presence of the king stated boldly, *"We want you to know, Your Majesty, that we will not serve your gods or worship the image of gold you have set up"* (Daniel 3:18).

Servant leaders take a stand for what is right, not for what they want or for what will benefit themselves. They do not wait on someone else to act or until public opinion is on their side. They hold firm convictions about right and wrong based on God's moral principles and boldly declare what they believe.

Humility enables a servant leader to trust the results to God. Daniel and his friends boldly took a stand for right, but at the same time humbly recognized that they were not responsible for the results. Daniel spoke wisely to his supervisor, offered a ten day test, and then humbly trusted God for the results. The three men, when challenged by the king, refused to defend themselves. *"King Nebuchadnezzar, we do not need to defend ourselves before you in this matter"* (Daniel 3:16). They anticipated God's deliverance, but humbly trusted the results to God, acknowledging that even if God did not deliver them, their response would be the same. (See Daniel 3:18).

Many leaders only take a bold stand after carefully concluding that their chances for success are high. Servant leaders take a bold stand based on principle and humbly leave the results to God.

Leaders who are passionate for a moral cause often act boldly but at the same time arrogantly look down on those who disagree and are defensive and argumentative.

p. 32

Servant leaders speak for God and what is right but are not defensive since they trust God for the results.

Servant leaders, like Daniel and his friends, boldly stand for what is right and humbly trust the results to God. As they do, God uses them to accomplish His purposes for their nation.

For further reflection and discussion:

1. Read the story of Daniel and his friends (Daniel 1, 3, and 6) looking for ways that they demonstrated bold humility. What more do you learn from their story?

2. When is the last time you stood against the crowd? Reflect on that experience in light of Daniel's example. What did you do well? What could have been done better?

3. When it comes to moral issues, is your natural tendency boldness or humility? In what ways is God calling you to balance these two principles?

4. What are the significant moral issues facing you as a leader in your family, business, community, or nation?

5. What reasons can you easily give to avoid taking a stand?

6. What does it mean for you to stand for what is right?

7. What might God be calling you to do in response to these issues?

8. What would bold yet humble leadership look like in this situation?

7. PROFILES IN BOLD HUMILITY: NEHEMIAH

Why would a servant leader throw someone's household possessions on the street? Ask Nehemiah! *"I was greatly displeased and threw all Tobiah's household goods out of the room"* (Nehemiah 13:8). This is not a picture of a weak, passive leader. Nor is it an example of an angry dictator. Nehemiah is another picture of the tension great servant leaders balance between boldness and humility. In what ways does Nehemiah demonstrate both?

Boldness requires a servant leader to confront corporate wrong. Nehemiah's action against Tobiah was a bold confrontation of wrong. Tobiah had taken advantage of his relationship with the priest for selfish gain. This is not the only time Nehemiah boldly confronted wrong. When the people were taking advantage of the poor, he became angry, called a meeting, and demanded a change (Nehemiah 5:1-13). When they were guilty of working on the Sabbath, he closed the doors and stationed guards to change the practice, even threatening to "lay hands on" those who violated his instruction (Nehemiah 13:15-22). When the people intermarried with foreigners, Nehemiah rebuked them, beat them, and pulled out their beards! (Nehemiah 13: 23-27). (I do not recommend that you try all of his tactics, but we can all follow his example of boldly confronting corporate wrong!)

Servant leaders have courage to confront the sin of those they lead. Their leadership is based on clear moral principles, not on popular opinion. Like Nehemiah, they confront wrong with a motive to correct and to change, not to destroy or take personal revenge. At home, in the office, on the job, or in the church, servant leaders see themselves as representatives of God's Kingdom and speak out boldly when they see violations of His will. This is not a personal battle, or retaliation against those who resist them. Servant leaders confront wrong only in response to clear disobedience of God's will. But then they confront the wrong with boldness.

Humility enables a servant leader to confess personal wrong. The boldness of Nehemiah to confront corporate wrong flowed from his earlier confession of personal wrong. His story begins with a prayer of humble confession in which he confesses both his own sin and the sins of his people (Nehemiah 1:5-11). Later, when he called the people to repent and turn back to God, he was the first to sign the document of confession and renewal (Nehemiah 10:1).

Some leaders boldly confront the sins of others, but are unwilling to deal with their own. Jesus compared these leaders to one who focuses on a speck of sawdust in other people's eyes, while missing the plank in their own (Matthew 7:3-5). Servant leaders quickly acknowledge their own weakness and their continued need for God's grace. They do not wait for their sin to be exposed and then quickly issue a public apology. Instead, they allow God to search their hearts and humbly acknowledge the sin exposed there. Seeing our own sin and acknowledging our own need for God's grace allows us to extend the same grace and freedom to others. We are able to confront boldly yet with a deep humility instead of pride.

This humility forms the foundation from which a servant leader can boldly confront the sin of others. Only when personal sin is confessed does a servant leader have the moral authority to confront sin in others. When personal sin is first acknowledged, confrontation of corporate sin is done in a spirit of humility rather than pride.

Confrontation of corporate wrong without humility leads to chaos and rebellion. Humble confession of personal sins without confrontation of corporate sins does not lead to change. But when servant leaders combine humble confession of personal sin with bold confrontation of corporate sin, genuine transformation of individuals and the community is made possible. Let's lead with bold humility like Nehemiah!

For further reflection and discussion:

1. Read the entire story of Nehemiah's leadership, looking for other examples of his boldness and humility. In what ways does his life instruct the way you lead?

2. Which comes most naturally to you as a leader, boldly confronting wrong or humbly confessing wrong? What happens when one is not balanced by the other?

3. Have you experienced a situation in which a leader boldly confronted wrong but lacked personal humility?

   What was the result and what can you learn from this leader?

4. On the other hand, have you experienced the situation in which a leader had great humility but lacked the boldness to confront wrong in others? What was the result and what can you learn from this experience?

5. Are there current sins in your own life which need confession before you look at others?

6. In the group you lead are there corporate sins which need bold confrontation? If so, what are they?

8. PROFILES IN BOLD HUMILITY: PETER

The first message preached by Peter was confrontational and courageous and brought him into immediate conflict with the authorities. After his case was heard he left the court and gathered together with other believers and prayed, *"Now, Lord, consider their threats and enable your servants to speak your word with great boldness"* (Acts 4:29). His prayer reveals the balance of boldness and humility every servant leader needs and calls us to proclaim truth with humility.

Boldness releases a servant leader to proclaim God's truth. At risk to his own life, Peter boldly proclaimed truth to a hostile audience. He exposed their sin and called them to repentance and change (see Acts 3). The authorities responded quickly with force and threats and Peter is called to face their charges. These were the men who orchestrated the death of Jesus only a short time earlier. Even in this situation Peter continues to respond with boldness and ultimately refuses to obey their order to stop talking about Jesus! He proclaimed the truth of God in that situation seemingly without regard to what it might cost him.

Servant leaders have courage to speak the truth even in costly situations. They do not wait for everyone to approve since they are not seeking approval from others. They recognize that true leadership is not a popularity contest. Like Peter, they focus on God's agenda not their own. In the boardroom, pulpit, staff meeting, the teachers' lounge, or over a meal, servant leaders are not afraid to tackle tough issues. They are not bound by the desire to please people or to be politically correct. Their confrontation often cuts across the status quo and boldly calls people to change. When is the last time you boldly spoke truth?

Humility requires a servant leader to seek God's power. It is not difficult to think of Peter as bold, however, humility is not a word we would quickly associate with his leadership! But his prayer reveals that he was no longer relying on his natural leadership abilities for boldness but on God's strength. Perhaps he recalled his betrayal of Jesus and how he lacked the courage to speak truth in that situation. He had always been quick to speak but at that point realized that his natural leadership abilities were not enough. In this prayer he humbly acknowledges that on his own he did not have the courage needed to keep speaking in the face of the threat of death or imprisonment. He humbly sought and received God's power.

Those gifted to lead often assume that they have the power to change others. But servant leaders humbly acknowledge their own limitations and lack of ability to bring about a change of heart. Even those naturally gifted in leadership, like Peter, recognize that on their own they cannot produce positive change. They humbly seek God's power to fill them again and again. When is the last time you asked God for boldness?

When leaders are bold, but not humble, they do more harm than good. They confront situations with arrogance and a superior attitude, recklessly leading change. When leaders are humble, but not bold, no change takes place. Wrong is not confronted and truth is not revealed. Servant leaders learn from Peter to be bold and humble. This combination leads to the transformation of lives in those we lead. This is not learned from reading a book on leadership or by setting high goals for achievement. It comes by being with Jesus. The authorities could only explain the amazing courage of Peter by recognizing that he had been with Jesus. Servant leaders walk closely enough to Jesus to be set free from the need for praise from men. They are close enough to His heart to recognize situations that call for a proclamation of truth. From Him they gain passion to see God's Kingdom established in their home, their business, their church, and their world. When that happens, servant leaders rise up and lead with bold humility.

For further reflection and discussion:

1. Read Acts 3 and 4 and reflect on Peter's bold humility. What additional things can you learn from his example?

2. In what way is God asking you to follow Peter's example?

3. In your leadership, do you tend to lead with boldness or humility? What is the result?

4. What steps can you take to bring balance to your leadership in these areas?

5. What situations in your home, workplace, or church does God want to change?

6. Have you prayed enough about this situation to lead with bold humility? What will bold humility look like in this situation?

9. PROFILES IN BOLD HUMILITY: PAUL

Confrontation is one of the most difficult and painful tasks of leadership and Paul didn't like confrontation any better than we do. But when he recognized Peter's hypocrisy Paul didn't hold back. *When Peter came to Antioch, I opposed him to his face, because he was clearly in the wrong* (Galatians 2:11). Paul's rebuke was both bold and humble and serves as a guide to all servant leaders of how to effectively confront when it is needed.

Boldness enables personal confrontation. It took great courage for Paul to confront Peter. In the last chapter, we examined Peter who boldly confronted the religious leaders as the church was born. He was the spokesperson for the church, and Paul was a latecomer to the leadership team. Paul did not have seniority or position over Peter. All these factors make Paul's courage more remarkable. But he did it boldly and in this case, publically.

It takes courage to confront sin in another person's life and many leaders shrink from this task. Some hope that the problem will go away with time or that someone else will do the difficult task of confrontation. Some cultures find it more difficult to confront, especially when the confrontation is directed at someone in a higher position. But Paul's boldness lay in his understanding of the issues involved and his genuine love for Peter. Peter's hypocrisy threatened to destroy the power of the Gospel to break down barriers between Jews and Gentiles. It was a sin issue, not personal preference or opinion. Servant leaders can absorb personal insults and accusations, but when sin is involved, they need courage to confront. However, they confront to bring change, nor for personal revenge or vindication. Paul was not trying to undermine Peter's leadership or to take his position. It was not a personality fight or an attempt to make himself look good by making Peter look bad. Paul genuinely cared for Peter and wanted the best for him. Servant leaders love enough to speak out rather than ignoring the problem. They humbly desire the best for those they serve. When this calls for confrontation, they do so boldly.

Humility brings perspective to the confrontation. Paul boldly confronted Peter, but he did so with humility and love. His intent was to correct and build, not to destroy. Just a few chapters later Paul reminds all servant leaders, *Brothers and sisters, if someone is caught in a sin, you who live by the Spirit should restore that person gently. But watch yourselves, or you also may be tempted* (Galatians 6:1). Paul teaches servant leaders that the goal of confrontation is restoration, and for that to happen, it must be done gently. Servant leaders humbly recognize that even when they are called to confront, they themselves are far from perfect and acknowledge that they could easily be on the other end of the confrontation. Because they have experienced God's grace, they invite others to receive His grace. Their goal is to restore, not to destroy. This perspective radically alters both the content and spirit of the confrontation. If confrontation is done with the intent to prove the other person wrong, to vindicate oneself, to shame another, or instill fear in others, the outcome will not be redemptive. The spirit in which confrontation is done often determines the outcome.

Some leaders are bold and don't fear confronting others. But they do it with arrogance and pride which almost always leads to conflict. Other leaders are so "humble" they never confront with courage. Again, no change happens. Servant leaders are called to confront boldly but with the perspective of humility. When both are present, there is great potential that the confrontation will bring a positive change of heart. But regardless of the outcome, servant leaders approach confrontation with bold humility.

For further reflection and discussion:

1. In my leadership, do I more naturally confront wrong or avoid conflict? What is the result?

   What is God calling me to change?

2. Reflect on the last time you confronted someone. Did you do it with a spirit of humility? (If not, you likely need to go back and repent!) Was the issue you confronted a sin or just a difference of opinion between you and that person?

3. What current relationship in your leadership needs confrontation?

4. What are the reasons you have not already confronted?

5. What does Paul's example teach you and what is the step you need to take this week?

6. In what way is confrontation an expression of love?

7. Does lack of love lead you to avoid confrontation or to do it with the wrong perspective?

8. In what way does your culture influence confrontation?

9. In what ways does Paul's example speak specifically to your culture?

10. In this example, Paul's rebuke was public. When is this needed and when is it best to confront privately?

10. PROFILES IN BOLD HUMILITY: TIMOTHY

In the last chapter of this series we'll examine the life of Timothy, a young leader who was learning to balance boldness and humility through the mentoring of his spiritual father, Paul. He encouraged Timothy to be bold, especially as it related to his willingness to share with others the Good News of Jesus and to humbly accept the suffering it would bring. *For this reason I remind you to fan into flame the gift of God, which is in you through the laying on of my hands. For God did not give us a spirit of timidity, but a spirit of power, of love and of self-discipline. So do not be ashamed to testify about our Lord, or ashamed of me his prisoner. Rather join with me in suffering for the gospel, by the power of God* (2Timothy 1:6-8).

Servant leaders boldly present Jesus to others. Paul encourages Timothy not to be timid in testifying about the Lord, but bold. Perhaps Timothy had a timid personality or simply didn't enjoy talking much. In any case, Paul encouraged him to *"fan into flame"* the gifts God had entrusted to him and to receive the boldness God desires for all leaders. He challenged Timothy not to be ashamed of the Gospel, but to declare if fearlessly. No matter where we live in the world it takes boldness to publically share Jesus with others. Communicating the Gospel always elicits spiritual opposition which requires leaders of courage to overcome it. Servant leaders seek to model their faith in all they do but they do not shrink from sharing verbally about Jesus. They pray for opportunities to share Jesus with their employees, co-workers, customers, neighbors, family members, and friends. Speaking about issues of faith in the public arena requires leaders of courage who are filled with the Spirit of God. Boldness in sharing is not measured in the volume of our speech, but in our willingness to speak clearly and with conviction when required. Servant leaders recognize that God has placed them in positions of influence to speak for Him.

Servant leaders humbly accept suffering for the Gospel. Paul challenges Timothy to boldly proclaim the Good News of Jesus and then quickly invites him to join in suffering for the sake of the same Gospel. Bold sharing is coupled with humble acceptance of suffering by servant leaders. They expect resistance to the message of the Gospel. At times this may be in the form of physical opposition; at other times the resistance is much more subtle. Leaders who speak boldly may be mocked or accused of being intolerant, narrow minded, or old fashioned. Servant leaders share boldly but do not fight to be heard or insist on defending themselves or their message. They refuse to be drawn into arguments or defend their own 'rights' to be heard and understood. They recognize that the message is not about them and they are simply chosen by God to deliver it to those God brings into their lives. They rejoice when the message is welcomed but they persevere when it is rejected. They will not stop sharing even when it costs them prestige in the eyes of others, a business deal, customers, friends, or finances. They look to Jesus who suffered and acknowledge that His followers are called to join with Him in suffering. Paul, often beaten and imprisoned for the sake of the Gospel, calls Timothy and all servant leaders to humbly accept suffering as part of our leadership. We seek to balance bold humility as we share our faith. When servant leaders find that they are not experiencing any suffering, they cry out for more boldness!

In the preceding chapters we have reflected on the call for servant leaders to possess confident **boldness** balanced with deep **humility**. Timothy, and the other leaders we have examined, teach us that it *is* possible to balance the two. May we each rise up and lead...with bold humility!

For further reflection and discussion:

1. Would others describe me as "bold" or "timid" in sharing the Gospel? What is the result in my leadership?

2. Where does a leader receive the boldness Paul challenged Timothy to have? What does Acts 1:8 have to say to this question?

3. Who are the people Christ has put in my life with whom I can share the Gospel?

4. In what ways have I been faithful to that calling and in what ways have I neglected the calling?

5. What types of opposition have I faced in sharing the Gospel?

    Has it diminished my boldness in any way?

6. What is God speaking to me in regard to opposition?

11. LEADERSHIP AND MINISTRY

I met a man walking in the park one day and we struck up a conversation. When he learned that I was a Christian he excitedly told me about his pastor. "He's such a great guy. He's such a perfectionist he won't even let anyone else help with the bulletin." Before I could offer him some leadership training he continued, "I'm not such a great Christian, but my pastor says that's okay because if I was, I wouldn't need him!"

Leadership and ministry are distinct. This pastor, like many Christian leaders, believes that his job is to work hard and serve the rest of the church. This is a noble intent, but this is *not leadership*, it is *ministry*. What's the difference? *Ministry* is doing the 'stuff' of the church or organization. It's producing the bulletins, visiting the sick, counseling, encouraging, setting up the chairs, working on the budget etc. *Leadership* is a different issue altogether. Paul says clearly that leaders in the church are supposed to equip others to do the work, *to prepare God's people for works of service...* (Eph. 4:12). *Leadership* is providing direction, motivation, and training that empowers and develops others.

Servant leaders serve by leading not by working.
This concept is especially tough for servant leaders.
Aren't we supposed to serve others? Absolutely! But we
can serve others by doing the work of *ministry* or by
providing Godly *leadership*. It's the difference between
coaching the team and *playing* the game. Even if a coach
is an excellent player, he would be foolish to get on the
field and play. The team needs a coach and he serves the
players by providing the leadership they need. Jesus led
with the heart of a servant, but he didn't do all the
serving! Servant leaders are focused on the needs of the
followers and will meet their needs. But they serve by
directing instead of doing.

Does this mean a servant leader shouldn't do any
ministry work? Of course not! As a part of the body of
Christ he/she will also do the 'work of ministry.' But the
leader should understand that while every believer is
called to do *ministry*, only leaders will provide the
direction that is needed for the body to move forward. If
the leader only ministers, who will lead? With the heart
of a servant they don't refuse to work or feel that the
work is beneath their dignity. But they also know they
are called by God to lead!

Why is this such a difficult concept? *Ministry* is
easier than *leadership* and more quickly feeds our ego
with immediate results. Further, most leaders have been
trained for ministry, not leadership, and find it difficult to
know how Christian leadership should be expressed.

Do you serve by ministering, or do you serve by
leading?

For further reflection and discussion:

1. What have you experienced as a leadership model...a minister/worker or a leader?

   How has that impacted your view of leadership?

2. What are other reasons that it is more difficult to lead than to 'minister' or do the work?

3. What percentage of your time currently goes to ministry and what percentage is leadership?

   What would you like it to be?

   What needs to change?

4. In what way are you currently providing leadership at home, in your vocation, and in your church?

12. ADVANCE THROUGH RETREAT

Leaders are by nature action-oriented and assume that doing more equals achieving more. But servant leaders learn the power of retreating from Jesus, the master leader. Mark records a profound incident during a busy season of Jesus' ministry. *Then, because so many people were coming and going that they did not even have a chance to eat, he said to them, "Come with me by yourselves to a quiet place and get some rest." So they went away by themselves in a boat to a solitary place* (Mark 6:31-32).

The situation facing Jesus has all the marks of success. People are "coming and going." There was so much work that there was no time for food. This is exactly what leaders dream about! The church is filled with people; the business has customers waiting in line; the speaking invitations are pouring in and everyone is asking to see you! There's not enough time to answer all the calls or respond to all the emails.

But in the midst of all this activity, Jesus tells the disciples to come away and rest. I suspect the disciples walked towards the boat shaking their heads in disbelief.

How could Jesus ask them to stop at the height of their popularity? How can you serve people when you retreat? Retreating helps leaders advance in several ways.

Retreat provides perspective. Getting away always produces a different perspective on life and works just like looking at the ground from a tall building or airplane. The big picture is easier to see. We find the true meaning of our labor and realize the true size of our problems. We recognize that the things we are investing heavily in are good, but not the best. We acknowledge our human limitations. Quiet reflection brings a fresh perspective to all we do.

Retreat sharpens our focus. When there are many things demanding our time and attention we lose focus. Priorities are blurred and we spend energy on less significant activities. The cry of the urgent quiets the voice of the important. Retreat helps us recognize when we have allowed our ministry, work, or business to take precedence over more significant relationships with God and family. We are able to refocus on the most important relationships and the most productive activities.

Retreat replenishes our strength. As we find God's perspective and regain focus we are able to return to the context of our work with renewed energy and vitality. Exhaustion is replaced with energy through retreat.

Servant leaders need times of retreat if they will continue to effectively meet the needs of those who follow. God graciously established in the laws of nature a time for rest and retreat. The Sabbath is a weekly time to refocus and be renewed that servant leaders learn to utilize. Seasons and years mark the passing of time and create points of reference for evaluation and reflection. Introverted personalities more quickly recognize their need for retreat and naturally are drawn to quiet times for reflection and renewal. Extroverted personalities find it harder to see the need for retreat and practice the discipline of rest. But Jesus still calls *all* of His disciples to advance through retreat. Are you willing to hear His call and walk away from the crowds to a quiet place?

For further reflection and discussion:

1. When is the last time you turned off your phone and got away from all activity to retreat?

2. Have you established a rhythm of times to retreat weekly? Seasonally? If not, look at your calendar now and start planning!

3. How does your personality encourage or discourage retreat?

4. When you do not retreat, what are the warning signs in your leadership?

13. DON'T TELL ME, SHOW ME

Servant leaders influence others by modeling the way. Leadership is more about showing than it is about telling and those who model the way shape lives. Think of those we call 'role models' from the media or sports. Their actions influence millions, for good or for bad. Paul's life is a great example of a servant leader who modeled the way. He said boldly, *"Follow my example, as I follow the example of Christ"* (1 Corinthians 11:1).

Paul modeled by default. Even without deliberate effort, Paul's life and leadership was a model to others simply because he passionately followed Christ. Paul had a passion to know Christ and to walk in obedience to His call. Servant leaders must first of all be followers of Jesus…at home, in the office, in the marketplace, and in ministry. Does the life you live quietly challenge others to be more like Christ?

Paul modeled by design. Paul not only modeled the way by default, but he deliberately called others to imitate him. *"Follow me…"* Can you say to those who follow you, "Do what I do…keep accounts like I do, love like I do, give your time like I do, work like I do, love your spouse like I do," etc.?

How can we be leaders worth imitating? First work

on the inside…then call for others to imitate you.

Take personal inventory. Carefully examine your own life, especially in the area of character. Use the questions below as a starting point. What is God calling you to change?

Eliminate stumbling blocks. After taking a personal inventory, identify the areas that most significantly impact your ability to be a model to others. Develop a plan to eliminate these from your life. This may require sharing them with a spouse, good friend, or mentor for prayer and accountability. You might find it helpful to memorize Scriptures dealing with the area in which you are working. Set realistic goals and allow the Spirit to work within you to produce change.

Take time to develop consistency. Be willing to allow God time to work on your life character as a leader. Consistency does not develop overnight; it is a lifelong process. This does not mean perfection or none of us would qualify. But even when we fail, our goal should be to model what it means to confess and forsake our sin.

After we have taken the other steps, we should, like Paul, consciously call others to follow our example. We may feel that this is exalting ourselves above others and certainly, the potential for this exists. But the example of Paul shows that it can be done as an effective form of leadership. Model the way, first by being a leader worth following; then call others to follow you.

For further reflection and discussion:

1. Take a personal inventory by asking yourself the
    questions below. Mark the ones which need more
    reflection and action.
    Is there a promise I made in the past month which
       I have not kept?
    Have I made a mistake for which I have not asked
       forgiveness?
    Are there ways in which I abuse my authority as a
       leader?
    Are there secret sins in my life that hinder my
       effectiveness as a leader?
    How am I growing in my intimacy with Jesus?
    Are there things I ask others to do that I am not
       willing to do?
    Have I responded in a timely manner to emails,
       calls, or requests from others?
    Do I have any broken relationships which I have
       not tried to rectify?
    Does my life exhibit more and more of the fruit of
       the Spirit?
    Do my leadership habits encourage others to be
       leaders?

2. From the list above, what action steps is God inviting you to make? Be specific and put the date you will begin.

3. Does calling others to imitate you mean that you are proud? Why or why not?

4. In what ways should you call others to imitate you?

14. THINKING FOR A CHANGE

Leadership is about seeing the need for and guiding the process of change. Management focuses on maintaining what exists, but leadership encourages change. However, change is uncomfortable and very few people enjoy change unless it is a change that we strongly desire (as when I changed my marital status from single to married!). Someone commented that the only people who truly enjoy change are wet babies! We naturally want to stay where we are, do the things we are already doing, and stay within our comfort zone. Paul calls all followers of Jesus to a life of continued change. *And we, who with unveiled faces all reflect the Lord's glory, are being transformed into his likeness with ever-increasing glory, which comes from the Lord, who is the Spirit* (2 Corinthians 3:18). What do servant leaders think about change?

Servant leaders see change as a part of growth. We need to change. Change is a part of growing and a natural part of life. All living things grow and change. Death comes when change stops. God wants us to grow and He wants those under our leadership to grow also. Servant leaders realize that change is a necessary part of growth and they guide others through the process of change. They understand that helping others change is essentially assisting them to develop all the potential God has placed within them. The workers in a business, the members in a church, or the staff in an office all have greater potential than they are currently using. A servant leader sees that potential and works to help them change and grow.

Servant leaders guide others through change. Servant leaders guide others through the process of change, but not just to feed their own ego or to build a name for themselves or the organization they lead. They are not interested in change for the sake of new things, to keep people occupied, or to create an appearance of activity. They lead change to develop people and to fulfill God's purposes for their lives and the organization. They recognize that not all change is healthy and that real growth is change in the right direction. In the process of leading positive change a church, business, or organization will naturally grow, but that is not the ultimate objective for a servant leader. The servant leader focuses on seeing followers change to become all God called them to be.

Servant leaders cast vision for change. They help others see the purpose of change. They cast vision to show the benefits of change in ways that motivate followers to pay the cost of change. The price of change is always high. It may not always be a financial cost; change may cost learning new ways of working together; it may cost learning a new leadership style; it may cost a loss of valued relationships or sense of community. Leaders are able to show that the cost is worth the effort.

Are you thinking for a change? Are you attentive to what God wants to change in you and through you? Serve others by leading change.

For further reflection and discussion:

1. In what ways am I currently growing?

2. What needs to change in my own leadership?

3. What will I do to begin or continue?

4. What needs to change in my organization?

5. What is the purpose of this change and what is God calling me to do to lead the change?

6. What is my motive for this change?

7. What obstacles will I meet in leading this change?

8. What price will need to be paid?

9. How will I persuade people that the price of change is worthwhile?

15. LEADING FOR A CHANGE

In the previous chapter, we examined the need to *think* about change. Now, let's talk about what it means to put those thoughts into action, *leading* for a change! The word CHANGE is a roadmap that will guide you as you lead change in your business, church, or community.

Communicate vision. Leaders share the vision with others, allowing them to see the need for change in a way that inspires action. They communicate clearly, convincingly, and continually. Servant leaders are honest about the cost of change and the results of failure to change but are also able to paint a compelling picture of what will happen when change is accomplished. They create a sense of need, urgency, and hope that things can be better. This hope is the great motivator that inspires action. Nehemiah is a great example. *Then I said to them, "You see the trouble we are in: Jerusalem lies in ruins, and its gates have been burned with fire. Come, let us rebuild the wall of Jerusalem, and we will no longer be in disgrace"(Nehemiah 2:17).*

Honor people. Servant leaders guide the process of change to develop others and to reach the objectives of the group, not simply to feed their own ambitions for success. They honor others in the process of change by recognizing those who invested in past changes and by identifying key influencers who will help bring change and allow them to influence those who respond more slowly.

Anticipate resistance. Servant leaders don't expect everyone to jump up and down when they announce change! Change is often accompanied by a fear of loss which may be loss of the familiar, a sense of identity, or loss of traditions and history. Look for it in advance, identify those who will be most likely to resist the change, and find ways to work with them.

Navigate the process. Leading change requires leaders who know where they are going and what steps will be required to get there. They communicate this process, get involved in it, and keep people focused on the goal as they move through the changes. Servant leaders not only develop a plan of action, but model the change and build momentum by beginning with small steps that show how things can improve and celebrating all victories.

Give time. True change always takes time and usually longer than the leader expects! Servant leaders recognize that it takes longer to lead through a change process than to begin something new, and they love people enough to patiently walk through the process.

Evaluate effectiveness. Good leaders are not afraid to ask tough questions to evaluate their effectiveness. Not only do servant leaders objectively measure success, but they are willing to ask if they have honored people in the change process.

Leaders are not needed to maintain the status quo; managers can handle that function. But when change is needed, servant leaders step up to the challenge, issue a call for change, and guide others through the process.

15. Leading for a Change

God will use you to bring change. Serve others by doing it well!

For further reflection and discussion:

1. What significant change is needed in my organization?

Now reflect on that change and answer the following questions.

2. Communicate Vision. How and when will I communicate the vision?

3. Honor people. In what specific ways will I seek to honor the people I am called to serve as I lead change?

4. Anticipate resistance. What challenges do I anticipate with this change?

5. Who are the people I expect to resist this change?

6. Navigate the process. What is my plan to implement this vision?

Is it clear enough to motivate others?

What is the first step?

7. Give time. How long do I expect this to take?

   Is this realistic?

8. Evaluate effectiveness. How and when will I evaluate?

   What will be the measure of success?

16. SERVANT LEADERS HAVE THE HOME FIELD ADVANTAGE

If you ask me about my leadership, I will quickly start talking about the organizations I've led, the number of people I've trained, or the good work I'm doing through my job. But servant leadership doesn't start on the *job*, it begins at *home*. Paul instructed Titus that a leader should be *the husband of but one wife, a man whose children believe and are not open to the charge of being wild and disobedient* (Titus 1:6). Politicians openly assert that what happens in their private lives has no bearing on their effectiveness as leaders, but Paul's guideline makes it clear that for servant leaders what happens at home is critical. Why?

Leadership at home is preparation for public leadership. Paul expects that before a leader exercises public influence, his or her leadership at home with spouse and children should be proven. If you can't influence those at home in a positive way, don't try to change the rest of the world! Leadership begins at home. A proverb from India says it well, "First win the home, then win the world."

At home, in the details of life, we learn to lead. We

learn to communicate and share vision, to plan and organize, strategize and execute, equip and build teams, and to negotiate and share. More than that, we develop character, the foundation of leadership, at home.

Nowhere is servant leadership more tested than at home. Servant leadership demands a surrender of personal rights and a focus on the needs of the other instead of self. This is difficult in public but nearly impossible at home without God's help! At home, we take off our nice clothes and relax. As we do so, we easily discard our good manners and people skills and begin to treat those closest to us in ways we would never do in public. It is impossible at home to hide who we really are. That's why learning to be a servant leader at home prepares us for public leadership.

While leadership at home should be proven, this does not imply perfection, or none of us would qualify. Instead, servant leaders learn to apologize and ask forgiveness for their mistakes, first at home and then in public.

Leadership at home is validation for public leadership. Not only does the home provide a learning environment for servant leadership, it also provides affirmation for our public leadership. Politicians may say that their private lives don't count, but they make sure that when it is time for pictures, their family is smiling beside them. Why? They know a smiling family sends a powerful message about leadership. It says to the voters, "You can't go wrong with this leader, look at the happy family!"

Paul recognized this as he challenged leaders 2000 years ago that their leadership at home confirms their ability to lead others. He understood that when a leaders' family is in order, the leader gains credibility in public. Servant leaders who have learned to lead well at home don't need to rely on fake smiles; they have genuine support from those who know them best. They stand with confidence and courage.

When a sports team plays at home, they possess the 'home field' advantage. Servant leaders who have paid the price at home have the 'home field' advantage when they enter the public arena.

Lead on….at home!

For further reflection and discussion:

1. On a scale of 1 to 10, how would your family rate your leadership?

   Now ask them and see what their response is!

2. What do you need to do at home to strengthen your leadership?

3. In your business/church/organization, what policies have you implemented that help to strengthen families?

4. Do you deliberately use your leadership to build families?

5. Are the families under your leadership growing?

6. What more can you do to strengthen them?

17. A LOVER OF GOOD

A folk proverb says, "Bad news travels fast." Pick up a newspaper or listen to the evening news and you'll quickly recognize that people gravitate toward bad news. But Paul tells Titus that a Christ-like leader should be *a lover of good* (Titus 1:8, NKJV). What does it mean to be a lover of good?

"A lover of good" speaks of our attitude...what we choose to think. Our attitude determines our direction in life and is a daily choice. We can choose to see the best or the worst; we choose to respond positively or negatively. Is the focus of your thoughts on good things or negative things? When you hear a report of the economy or political situation, do you choose to think about the difficulties or the opportunities?

Servant leaders choose to think about the good. Paul admonishes, *Finally, brothers, whatever is true, whatever is noble, whatever is right, whatever is pure, whatever is lovely, whatever is admirable-- if anything is excellent or praiseworthy-- think about such things* (Philippians 4:8).

"A lover of good" speaks of our focus...what we choose to highlight. Leaders have many opportunities to provide direction and continually choose what they will emphasize. Servant leaders choose to focus on the good in people or the situation. Paul writes that love *always hopes* (1 Corinthians 13:7). Effective leaders highlight the good.

When someone who reports to you makes a mistake, do you focus on the failure or the effort made? When you hear a negative report about someone, do you automatically assume that it is true or false? When developing others, do you focus on the strengths or weaknesses of the other? If you focus on the negative your leadership will be corrective. If you focus on strengths your leadership will be empowering. Servant leaders do not overlook the negative, but they highlight what is good. In doing so, they provide positive energy and direction and lead people out of negativity.

"A lover of good" speaks of our conduct...what we choose to do. If we love the good, our actions will reflect our thoughts and focus. Leaders who love good will continually choose good actions in their public and private lives. Peter urges, *Live such good lives among the pagans that, though they accuse you of doing wrong, they may see your good deeds and glorify God on the day he visits us* (1 Peter 2:12). As we practice good deeds, others will recognize that we are good workers, good citizens, good spouses, and good parents. Can others see by your actions that you love what is good?

The good news for servant leaders is that when you choose to be a lover of the good, good people love to follow! Bad news travels fast, but leaders who focus on the good last and last.

For further reflection and discussion:

1. Would you describe yourself as a lover of good?

   Would others?

2. What needs to change in your attitude? What steps can you take to make this change?

3. What good act can you choose to do today that will strengthen your ability to lead like Jesus?

18. MONEY MATTERS

Money matters to everyone. We all use money, need money, and handle money every day. Our money is a powerful force in our lives, and it is not surprising that the Bible has a lot to say about possessions and finances. The way a leader thinks about and handles money both reveals much about his or her heart and also powerfully impacts those who follow.

A servant leader is cautioned not to be a *lover of money* (1 Timothy 3:3). Paul's instruction deals not with how much money we have, but with our attitude towards it. Specifically, he cautions against an unhealthy appetite for money. How can we know if we 'love money?'

Choosing our vocation based on money. God calls servant leaders in the marketplace, in education, in the arts, and in church work. Each of these callings has monetary implications. For some, this means a business vocation that provides more than enough money, and in some cases, a special gifting to make money. For another, God's call may mean a life of sacrifice and seeming financial limitations. In either case, we cannot choose obedience if we are a *lover of money* and make career choices based on financial results instead of obedience. While God certainly has given every leader the responsibility to work hard and provide for their families, servant leaders seek to hear God's voice in their calling and to walk in obedience. How have you chosen to do what you do? Is it a calling or a decision based on finances? Is your objective to become financially secure or is it to maximize your gifts so others may benefit and see Jesus in your work and leadership?

Setting our priorities based on money. What is most important shapes our lives and determines our priorities. Leaders are faced daily with choices about priorities that determine the direction of their lives and those who follow. It is natural to focus on priorities that produce more money. In church planting, we can prioritize a higher class neighborhood rather than working with the poor. In a business, we can focus on short-term profitability rather than longer-term health or focus on profit over generosity towards employees.

Jesus' priority was clear; He focused on doing the will of His Father and taught that our first priority should be seeking the advancement of the Kingdom, not financial gain. Servant leaders focus on Kingdom priorities even when at the time it doesn't seem to be the best financial decision.

Making our decisions based on money. When our heart's desire is to have money, the daily decisions we make will reflect this passion. For business leaders, this often means maximizing return rather than serving the customer first or delivering a quality product. This is often referred to as putting the 'bottom line' first. Church leaders may decide who to visit based on the income level of the person involved or may be tempted to avoid preaching about certain issues for fear of offending a member with financial power.

Servant leaders look beyond these aspects and look at

broader objectives. They ask, "How will this decision benefit others, whether members, customers, or staff?" "What is God's desire for this situation and how can I act in a way that advances His Kingdom?"

What role does money play in your leadership? Are you a 'lover of money' or a servant leader with a radically renewed heart?

For further reflection and discussion:

1. In what unhealthy ways have I allowed money to impact my priorities and decisions?

2. What would those who follow me say about the way I view money?

3. Can you share a decision you made that was clearly not made on a financial basis?

19. MORE MONEY MATTERS

In the last chapter, we looked at what it means to not be a 'lover of money.' Now, we'll examine ways that servant leaders handle the money they have.

Servant leaders handle money as stewards. Servant leaders recognize that God has given to them many things, including their power of influence, gifts and abilities, and finances. Paul asks, *What do you have that you did not receive?* (1 Corinthians 4:7). Because they are servants, they handle these gifts, not as their own, but as stewards. When leaders view their finances as stewards, they recognize that money is a tool God has provided to carry out His purposes in and through their leadership. They ask, "God, what do you want to do with the money you've given me?"

Servant leaders handle money with integrity. Misuse of money has caused the downfall of many leaders. Servant leaders are careful to use money in ways that will not cause others to stumble. This includes wrongs such as exaggerating expenses, falsifying receipts, or using the organization's stationary for personal correspondence. But it goes beyond just avoiding sin. Servant leaders make an effort to ensure that their financial dealings are completely open and above reproach in the eyes of others. Paul, when working with money that was contributed by the church said, *We want to avoid any criticism of the way we administer this liberal gift. For we are taking pains to do what is right, not only in the eyes of the Lord but also in the eyes of men* (2 Corinthians 8:20, 21). When dealing with money, servant leaders ask not only "Is this right?" but also question, "Will this action seem right to others or will it cause them to stumble?"

Servant leaders handle money with faith. Servant leaders do not separate their faith and their finances; they handle money in a manner that expresses their faith. When money is in short supply, they exercise faith as they move forward with confidence that God will provide for what He has called them to do. They exercise faith when they are willing to give money away, even when it doesn't make economic sense. Servant leaders look at the balance sheet or financial report, but they also keep an ear open to hear God's instructions and have the courage to walk in obedience as stewards. God's instructions may be to give a few coins to a needy person, to put some money in savings for the future, or to give a huge sum towards His work. Faith means walking in obedience.

Your money matters...a lot! The way you use it affects your life and your leadership. Guard your heart from the love of money. Then use money as a steward with integrity and faith.

For further reflection and discussion:

1. Do I handle money as my own or as a steward?

2. What decisions have I made recently that reflect this?

3. What are my greatest areas of temptation in handling money?

4. What can I do to avoid any hint of suspicion in how I handle money?

5. In what ways is God calling me to express faith through money?

20. LEADING WITH AN OPEN HEART

All leaders influence followers, but only servant leaders open their hearts to those who follow. Paul, in an intimate letter to the Corinthian church said, *We have spoken freely to you, Corinthians, and opened wide our hearts to you* (2 Corinthians 6:11). Paul's statement reveals a deliberate action which he took to connect with his followers. Leading with an open heart is never an accident; it is always a deliberate choice made in spite of the potential for hurt which exists.

Leading with an open heart does not happen easily or naturally. Leadership positions tend to encourage a gap between leader and follower. Some leaders encourage this gap and deliberately ensure that they maintain an emotional distance from those they lead by keeping all relationships at a 'professional' level. Leaders face daily choices about how open they will be with those who follow and should recognize that the natural tendency is to cover up who we really are and what is in our hearts. Leading with an open heart is always a choice of the will that focuses on the needs of others instead of our own fears or insecurities.

Leading with an open heart is a powerful leadership act that greatly multiplies influence. Servant leaders are willing to expose their own needs and weaknesses in appropriate ways. This models an authenticity which helps genuine relationships to develop and flourish. Leadership is all about relationships, and as effective leaders open their hearts, they create an environment that feels safe for others to expose who they really are. This fosters an environment of trust and respect among staff persons or workers. Although relationships today are characterized by short text messages, one-line Facebook postings, and Twitter updates; there is still a deep longing in our hearts to connect at a more intimate level. Servant leaders take the initiative to make this happen by opening their hearts.

Leading with an open heart allows communication, not only of directives but of motives and reveals the 'why' behind the 'what.' For example, a servant leader can say, "I'm asking you to do this because I want to see you grow and develop." Further, leaders who open their heart consistently attempt to communicate all that is appropriate. There are certainly times that it is inappropriate to share all that is in your heart, but servant leaders make it a habit to be as open as possible.

Opening your heart to others is an enormous risk. You can be wounded deeply or misunderstood. Followers may not always quickly reciprocate. The context of Paul's statement reveals that his followers did not respond to his example in a like manner, at least not without some prodding from him. But if you desire to serve those you lead, it's worth the risk. Leaders who consistently open wide their hearts to others are powerfully attractive and unfortunately far too uncommon. Take a deliberate step today to join Paul by not just opening a small crack in your leadership heart, but opening it wide!

For further reflection and discussion:

1. Does my leadership encourage others to open up their hearts?

2. Has my leadership created a culture of openness in the organization I lead?

3. Have I experienced pain in the past that makes it more difficult for me to lead with an open heart?

   What do I need to do to find healing?

4. What specific action have I done in the last week that revealed an open heart? Or, where did I miss an opportunity to open my heart?

5. Have I found ways to appropriately reveal my own needs and expose my own weaknesses to those who follow me?

21. LEADING WITH EXCELLENCE

Servant leaders, like all great leaders, have a passion for excellence. However, their motive to lead with excellence is not simply for personal benefit or to increase financial revenue. Servant leaders lead with excellence because they have a passion to develop their own potential, to see others develop their potential, and a desire to reflect God's nature in their leadership. Paul challenges all of us, *Whatever you do, work at it with all your heart, as working for the Lord, not for men* (Colossians 3:23). His call is a challenge to rise above mediocrity to a wholehearted pursuit of excellence wherever we lead. What is the result when servants lead with excellence?

Leading with excellence reflects the nature of God. The God we serve is not a lukewarm, half-hearted, casual God. Whatever He does is the best and we are called to visibly express His nature in all we do.

This excellence is expressed in our vocations where we use the gifts and abilities God has given us for His glory. If that is in construction, build the best buildings possible. If it is in education, teach with a passion that produces excellence. If you are a pastor, be excellent! Martin Luther King Jr. expressed it well, "If it falls to your lot to be a street sweeper, sweep streets like Michelangelo painted pictures, like Shakespeare wrote poetry, like Beethoven composed music; sweep streets so well that all the hosts of heaven and earth will have to pause and say, 'Here lived a great sweeper, who swept his job well.'" As we lead and serve with excellence we reflect God's very nature.

Leading with excellence inspires the best from followers. Leaders who model excellence bring forth the best in their followers. Some leaders attempt to dictate good performance from followers and go to great lengths to measure this performance. But healthy leaders live and serve with excellence in a way that inspires others to also do their very best. Think about a leader that inspires you and reflect on what it is about their leadership that helps you to do better. Very likely they have a passion for excellence.

Leading with excellence increases results. Positive results can be expected when we lead with excellence. Results may be measured in the 'bottom line' of financial profit in a business or in the maturity of disciples or community impact for a church. In any case, when we lead and work with excellence, positive results normally follow. Given a choice between a mediocre product and an excellent one, which will you purchase? If you want to select a church, will you be attracted to one that doesn't care how things are done or one where attention is given to excellence? It only makes sense that we are attracted to excellence, and doing things God's way works! For this reason even an unbelieving leader who pursues excellence will see increased results. What distinguishes the servant leader is the motive behind the commitment to excellence. The servant leader pursues excellence as a means to expand the rule of God in his or her sphere of influence.

Servant leaders are passionate about being the best leaders they can to bring glory to God. Because of this they pursue excellence in all they do and continually grow in their leadership capacity.

For further reflection and discussion:

1. Do I consistently model excellence in all I do?

2. Does my leadership inspire excellence in others?

3. What is my motive for the pursuit of excellence?

4. What specific examples of excellence can others see in the organization I lead?

5. How can I respond to the call to excellence while avoiding unhealthy perfectionism?

22. MOSES: A BACKGROUND CHECK

In the next chapters, we'll reflect on the life and leadership of Moses. Why Moses? Consider these credentials. He was called the most humble man on the face of the earth and spoke to God face to face unlike any other prophet. He led a large group (likely over 2 million) for a period of 40 years and overcame all types of challenges including self-doubt, physical survival, external attacks, and internal dissension. In Hebrews he is listed in the faith "Hall of Fame" where more space is devoted to him than any other single leader. We have some things to learn from a servant leader like Moses! In this chapter, we'll examine key elements from his background that shaped his leadership.

He was born into a family of faith. Moses was born into a Hebrew family during difficult times and into a life of slavery and poverty. However, the strong faith of his parents enabled them to work hard to preserve his life from those who wanted to kill him, and with God's favor, his birth mother was able to raise him for some of his formative years. This experience shaped his life of faith.

He was adopted as a young child. After being nursed by his own mother, Moses went to live in the Egyptian palace as an adopted child of Pharaoh's daughter. He learned another language and another culture and was separated from his siblings. Living in a position of privilege did not spare Moses from the struggles of identity that many adopted children face. He must have often wrestled with the question of where he belonged and how to be loyal to his birth mother who nursed him and his adopted mother who named him.

He was well educated. As a child of the princess, Moses had the benefit of a world-class education and had the best of Egypt at his fingertips. He became *powerful in speech and action* (Acts 7:22).

What impact did Moses' background have on his leadership and what can we learn about servant leadership from his past?

God calls servant leaders from all backgrounds. Moses experienced a short time in a family of faith and years outside of that environment of faith. Yet, he emerges as a man of faith and a strong servant leader. Moses could have focused on his birth in poverty and slavery and felt unworthy to lead. He could have focused on his life of privilege and felt entitled to lead. With time, he did neither. You might be tempted to exalt your background or hide it, but Moses' life shows that your usefulness in leadership does not depend on whether you have gone to church all your life or if you grew up in rebellion towards God. Keep your background in the background as you focus on what God has called you to do.

God uses our background to shape us for service. While God can call you from any background, it is also clear that God uses our background to shape us for service in a specific context. Moses' early exposure to his faith heritage gave him the perspective he needed to turn his back on the privileged life of a prince. His adoption and years of separation from his birth family shaped the way he related to and cared for others. His time in the palace and his educational background uniquely equipped him to return to Pharaoh's court and ask for God's people to be released. He knew the protocol and language of the palace in ways that no other Hebrew could have known. Likewise, your background does not *qualify* you for service, but God does use it to *equip* you to serve.

Read the background scriptures below and reflect on how your background can be used of God to shape your place and style of leadership as a servant leader - Exodus 2:1-2; Hebrews 11:23-29; Numbers 12:3; Acts 7:17-44 and Deuteronomy 34:10.

For further reflection and discussion: for

1. What life experiences have significantly shaped the way I lead? (Reflect on your religious, educational, and social background)

2. How has God used my background to uniquely equip me to lead in my current place of service?

3. Do I tend to look down on my background or to exalt it? What is the result of an unhealthy focus on my past?

4. What is the background of my church or organization?

5. In what way has God uniquely shaped me to accomplish His purposes in this time and place?

23. MOSES: FIRST ATTEMPTS AT LEADERSHIP

Moses' first recorded leadership act was a disaster! *One day, after Moses had grown up, he went out to where his own people were and watched them at their hard labor. He saw an Egyptian beating a Hebrew, one of his own people. Glancing this way and that and seeing no one, he killed the Egyptian and hid him in the sand* (Exodus 2:11-12).

Perhaps Moses already knew that God had called him to rescue His people. At least his heart motive was to bring change, to set right the injustice he saw, and to see an end to the suffering of his people. He thought his people would recognize his call to lead, but they didn't. His action was decisive but he chose the wrong time and method. The result was that he had to flee for his life and spend 40 years in the desert before he was ready to try again. There are at least three ways that Moses' first attempts at leadership were not acts of a servant leader.

Moses acted independently. At this point in his life, Moses was ready to be the hero that single-handedly rescued his people. He had not yet learned the value of a team or what it means to work under authority. Moses must have imagined that it was going to be his effort and ability that would accomplish the task. But servant leadership is about working with and through people, not being a solitary hero. Servant leaders learn that leadership is not about them, their vision, and their ability as much as it is about learning to hear what God wants and moving people in that direction. Servant leaders are called to act, but they are not called to act independently of God's direction and the counsel of a wise team.

Moses acted impulsively. Moses saw the situation, made a decision to get involved, and killed the Egyptian in what appears to be a very short time. Leaders are oriented towards action; they want change and often want it now! But impulsive acts are often more destructive than helpful. Servant leaders are not only looking for action, but seeking the right action. They are willing to seek counsel and pray for wisdom before acting. They exhibit self-control, a fruit of the Spirit. They are action-oriented but not impulsive.

Moses acted secretly. Before he killed the Egyptian Moses looked around to ensure that no one was looking. Afterward, he used sand to cover what he had done. He knew it was wrong! Of course, he could rationalize it because of his good motives, but when your leadership act needs to be followed by a cover-up, reconsider! Servant leaders walk in openness and transparency. They are not making deals under the table or in dark corners. The goal for servant leaders is never to do anything that they would be ashamed to find on the front page of tomorrow's newspaper.

Moses tried hard, but he wasn't yet ready for the challenge of servant leadership. God would need to take him to the desert for the next level of leadership development, and in our next chapter we'll examine that step. But thank God that Moses' failed first attempts at leadership did not keep God from using him. Likewise, our first attempts at leadership do not need to be our final ones! God is merciful and still had a plan to use Moses and will continue shaping our leadership as well.

For further reflection and discussion:

1. Are there areas in my leadership in which I am acting independently of others?

   Independently of God?

2. When in my leadership have I acted impulsively?

3. What was the result and what can I learn from that mistake?

4. To what extent is my leadership characterized by self-control?

5. How can I allow God's Spirit to develop more self-control in my life? (See Galatians 5:22-23)

6. Have I made any decisions or taken any actions in the past week that I don't want others to know about?

7. Is there anything I am currently doing which would bring shame to the cause of Christ if it were publicized in tomorrow's newspaper?

24. MOSES: PREPARATION IN THE DESERT

Moses' life and leadership took a dramatic change after his first attempt at leadership. Pharaoh discovered what Moses had done and sought to kill him. So *Moses fled from Pharaoh and went to live in Midian... (Exodus 2:15b)*. Picture the transition. Moses goes from being *powerful in speech and action* (Acts 7:22) to being an unknown stranger in the desert. One day he was a privileged member of the ruling family in Egypt; the next, a fugitive on the run. One day he had servants at his disposal; the next day there was no one who paid any attention to his needs. For the next 40 years Moses lived in the desert as a shepherd as God prepared him to be a servant leader. As we observe what happened to Moses in the desert, we can gain valuable principles about how God prepares servant leaders.

Preparing servant leaders requires character development. Moses didn't become the meekest man on earth in the palace; he developed this characteristic in the desert. God took this time to strategically shape the character of Moses. In the desert his royal titles didn't matter. His ability to navigate the halls of the palace didn't help him find his way to the watering hole. His education at this point seems to have been wasted. It is a time of breaking and humbling for Moses. God is preparing him for the challenges of leading a nation where his character would be sorely tested. He needed to be able to handle miraculous power without pride; he would need to withstand tremendous opposition and rebellion without retaliation. This time of character training was so effective that in the rest of Moses' life and leadership, we only find one time when he failed in a test of his character. God shapes our character over time by allowing us to go through our own times of testing. He is more interested in a strong foundation than a polished exterior.

Preparing servant leaders requires acts of service. Moses had learned the art of taking life in Egypt. Now he needed to learn the skill of care and nurture. He learned to serve others, not through heroic actions, but through small acts of sacrifice. His heart to serve leads Moses to rescue the daughters of Midian and water their flocks. From that act God gives him a wife and then children, more great opportunities to learn to serve others! The act of shepherding for years must have taught Moses a lot about looking out for the needs of the sheep, protecting them from danger, finding food for their physical needs, and nurturing those who were weak or sick. Those whom God will use as servant leaders must learn how to serve others. Those who are not willing to pay the price of obscure acts of service are not capable of leading from the top with a servant's heart.

Preparing servant leaders requires time. 40 years is a long time! Wasn't there a faster way for God to teach Moses all He wanted him to learn? We live in a modern world where we want instant results and expect leaders to develop quickly. But leadership development is a process that takes time, and there are no shortcuts for God's preparation process.

As harsh and uncomfortable as the desert must have been for Moses, it is the place God chose to prepare him. Many other biblical leaders including Elijah, David, Jesus and Paul spent transformational time in isolation. Leadership maturity is forged on the anvil of difficulty, and servant leaders allow God to complete His work in the desert.

After 40 years as a shepherd, Moses was ready for the call that would transform his life. We'll look at that in our next chapter.

For further reflection and discussion:

1. Are there areas of your leadership in which you sense that the foundation is not strong enough to support the role you are carrying?

2. What can you learn from Moses' preparation that can help you?

3. If you sense that you are in a stage of preparation for leadership, reflect on what God is doing.

4. What areas of character is He working on in your life?

5. What acts of service is He calling you to do that will go unnoticed by others?

6. Read the accounts of other Biblical leaders who had wilderness experiences in 1 Kings 19; 2 Samuel 1, Matthew 4, and Galatians 1:17-18. What do you learn from their experience that is helpful for your own leadership?

25. MOSES: A CLOSE CALL

After 40 years tending sheep in the desert, God calls Moses to lead His people out of Egypt. God uses a burning bush to get Moses' attention. The dramatic experience recorded in Exodus 3:1-4:31 provides a framework for God's call to all servant leaders.

God calls those He has prepared. God's call to Moses came after 40 years of shaping in the wilderness. Moses' first attempts at leadership revealed that he had much to learn. After 40 years of desert training, Moses was prepared for action. He had been humbled and learned the discipline of hard work. His excellent academic training was now balanced with on-the-job experience. Moses was prepared for the call.

God calls those who are active. God called Moses while he was on the job. He was busy with his daily duties, faithfully working as a shepherd and meeting the needs of his family. In this position, God called him. Some leaders sit around waiting for their big opportunity to appear, but God delights in using people who are already being faithful at what they are doing.

God calls leaders first to Himself. Servant leadership begins with a personal relationship with God. God was seeking Moses' attention through the burning bush and responded quickly when Moses turned toward Him. This initial encounter marked the beginning of a face-to-face relationship with God which would mark Moses' leadership. While we may not experience a burning bush, any leadership that does not flow out of the foundation of an encounter with God is not servant leadership. Jesus called His disciples to be *with* Him before He sent them out to preach (Mark 3:14). God desires relationship more than service and invites all of us into His presence. In His presence, we understand His love and the work to which He has called us. This is truly a close call.

God's call meets a human need. God's call to Moses clearly was in response to the plight of His people who were suffering in Egypt. God always calls servant leaders to fulfill a part of His plan for the world, meeting the needs of His people. Whether you serve in church leadership, in your profession, or in a business, God's call upon your life is not just to supply your needs; it is to meet a specific need in His world. Reflect for a moment on how your leadership meets the needs of those around you.

God's call provokes a sense of inadequacy. As Moses began to understand the extent of God's call, he responds with a deep sense of inadequacy. *"Who am I, that I should go to Pharaoh and bring the Israelites out of Egypt?"* (Exodus 3:11). Moses is so broken after 40 years in the desert that he almost sees himself as incapable of leading. Yet, in this condition of self-doubt, Moses was more ready than earlier when he was confident in his own strength. Servant leaders learn to rely on God's strength to carry out the mission. Their confidence comes not from their own abilities but from the relationship they have with the One who calls them close. From this call flows the courageous leadership we'll examine in the next chapter.

For further reflection and discussion:

1. Are you confident of God's call on your leadership role?

2. If so, reflect on how this impacts your leadership. If not, what do you need to do to confirm His direction for your leadership?

3. Do you see your leadership primarily as a call to a relationship with Jesus, or as a call to act?

4. What difference does it make in the way you lead?

5. Do you feel humanly adequate for what God has called you to do?

6. How does Moses' encounter with God help you?

7. Do you find it easy to lead from your own strengths instead of relying on God's provision and direction?

8. What does Moses' life teach you?

26. MOSES: LEADING WITH COURAGE

Afterwards Moses and Aaron went to Pharaoh and said..."Let my people go" (Exodus 5:1). With this simple sentence Moses begins what will be forty years of leadership. For Moses, and every servant leader, after the call from God, there's work to be done! His entrance into Pharaoh's court is a lesson in courage for each of us.

Reflect with me for a moment on why this was a courageous act. First, Moses was reentering Egypt where forty years earlier he fled as a fugitive. His name was surely still on the government list of wanted men, but he boldly entered and headed straight to the capital city! Secondly, he displayed courage by entering the office of the strongest leader in the world at that time. Shepherds don't usually have the courage to walk in those corridors. Finally, Moses' courage was revealed in his bold request, "Let my people go." He was not asking for a small favor; he was suggesting that Pharaoh give up his economic engine. What can we learn from the courage of Moses?

Courage flows out of God's call. Moses' encounter with God in the desert convinced him that he was called by God to lead the people out of Egypt and provided the courage he needed to face Pharaoh. Moses' courage did not come from his own abilities since the forty years in the desert left him as a broken man. He left Egypt mighty in speech and aware of his own abilities, but now he returns as a man called by God. When he murdered the Egyptian forty years earlier he had physical strength; he now returns with moral courage. It was God's call that made the difference in his life and which empowers all servant leaders.

To think about: Do I sense God's call in what I am doing to the extent that I have the needed courage to fulfill that call?

Courage focuses on God's mission. Moses found courage by focusing on the mission or work to which God called him. He was not back in Egypt to see the pyramids; he had a mission to accomplish. His people were in bondage and suffering at the hands of Pharaoh. But Moses could see his people as a free nation; free to live where they pleased and free to worship as God desired, and he knew that his task was to lead the people to this goal. It was not Moses' mission; it was God's, and that focus enabled Moses to move with courage. Focusing on a mission larger than our own interests instills a sense of purpose and courage. Many leaders often lack courage because their focus is on their own small mission of selfish gain. Servant leaders are not bullies seeking to push their own agenda. Instead, their courage comes from God's mission, and they are not timid about pushing His agenda.

To think about: Do I focus on God's mission in my leadership or my own agenda?

Leadership requires courage. It takes courage to stand when no one else is standing. It takes courage to call people to commit themselves to a cause bigger than themselves. Leadership is not for the faint of heart. Servant leaders, like Moses, do not find courage in who they are or their own agendas. Rather, they find courage in their sense of calling and a clear focus on the mission for which God brought them into leadership. Their courage is based on conviction rather than conceit. It inspires confidence in those they lead and keeps moving forward even when obstacles arise. We'll look more at this persistence in our next chapter.

For further reflection and discussion:

1. What issues in my leadership right now need courage?

2. What can I apply from Moses' leadership to my own journey?

3. As a follower, what is my natural response when I sense courage in a leader?

4. What does that teach me about my own leadership?

5. What has been the result in my leadership when I lacked courage?

   Was it because of my own fears and/or insecurities?

6. Do I have a clear sense of God's call and mission or am I focused on my own agenda?

27. MOSES: LEADING WITH PERSISTENCE

Pharaoh said, "Who is the Lord, that I should obey him and let Israel go? I do not know the Lord and I will not let Israel go" (Exodus 5:2). Moses is only three minutes into his leadership journey when he faces opposition! This opposition from Pharaoh goes on for weeks as God brings the ten plagues upon the land of Egypt. As if this was not enough, even the people Moses was trying to help refused to listen to him (Exodus 6:9). It's one thing to begin with courage, it's quite another to keep going when all kinds of opposition arise. It takes persistence to keep going when the going is tough and servant leaders learn from Moses' example how to lead with persistence.

Leading with persistence requires help. It doesn't take long after Moses' first encounter with Pharaoh before he returned to the Lord and said, *"Oh Lord, why have you brought trouble upon this people? Is this why you sent me?"* (Exodus 5:22). Moses knows he needs help to keep going and turns to the source of his call and vision, God himself. As the plot continues to unfold Moses learns that leading with perseverance is emotionally draining when he becomes "hot with anger" as he leaves Pharaoh's palace (Exodus 11:8). Moses is not immune to the immense toll that leadership takes on men and women who lead in difficult times. Like Moses, servant leaders are not afraid to admit that they need the help of God and others around them. They deliberately seek God's counsel and share their questions appropriately with mentors and colleagues.

Leading with persistence demands a long term view. To make it through these difficult days of the plagues Moses had to keep focused on the future. God reminded Moses repeatedly of His promise to bring the people out of Egypt. This vision of the future enabled Moses to persevere through the many conversations with Pharaoh, broken promises, dashed hopes, and all the ten plagues. Followers focus on the immediate problems but leaders keep their focus on the vision of where they are going. If you are leading through a difficult economic time or a time when people are leaving instead of joining your cause, look again at the long-term view. Servant leaders find strength in reminding themselves what God wants to do in the future.

Leading with persistence produces victory. Through all the ten plagues, Moses just kept moving forward. He went from Pharaoh's palace to the assembly of leaders and back again to the palace. It took time and many major events before Pharaoh's heart was changed with the death of his son but finally, after seven chapters of struggle, God's people are set free from Egypt. Victory didn't come on the first round or even the fifth but it came as Moses persistently followed God's direction and refused to give up. What if Moses would have given up in despair when the seventh plague didn't bring the change for which he hoped? He understood that some leadership challenges take a long time to win and require leaders who refuse to give up. Servant leaders are able to keep leading until the victory is accomplished.

If you're facing a leadership challenge and have felt like giving up, learn from the leadership of Moses that good things happen to leaders who do not quit. Ask for help, keep the long-term view in mind, and keep going until you see the victory. In the next chapter, we'll learn from Moses about celebrating those victories.

For further reflection and discussion:

1. Where do you turn for the help you need as a leader?

2. Have you developed a close group of friends to whom you can go when facing difficult leadership challenges?

3. Are you quick to turn to God for direction, like Moses?

4. Are you able to know when you have reached the end of your emotional reserves?

5. What are the signals that alert you that you are drained?

6. Do you normally focus on the short term obstacles or the long term vision?

28. MOSES: LEADING BY CELEBRATION

Victory at last! After leading with courage and persistence and going through all the drama of the 10 plagues, Moses finally leads the people out of Egypt. But almost as soon as they left the land of their slavery they were faced with the army of Pharaoh who had changed his mind about releasing his free work force. Soon Moses and the people were trapped between Pharaoh's army and the Red Sea with no means of escape. But God performed yet another miracle and opened up the sea for them to cross on dry land. The army of Pharaoh tried to follow them but were all destroyed in the water. After this great victory, Moses led the Israelites in a song of victory and a time of celebration. We can learn from the story in Exodus 15 how to lead with celebration.

Servant leaders initiate celebration. *Then Moses and the Israelites sang this song to the LORD...* (Exodus 15:1). We don't know if Moses was a great singer or musically challenged, but he led the group in a song of celebration. He didn't delegate the task to the celebration committee; he was on the front line! Leaders with vision often make the mistake of focusing only on the future and what is needed to get there. Moses knew that they were still not in the Promised Land. Nevertheless, a significant step towards that goal had been reached and he stopped the movement for a time to celebrate. This celebration didn't cost any money, but it did require a leader who called for time to celebrate. His example challenges us to stop at each significant victory and celebrate. Servant leaders recognize that when God brings success a celebration is in order. Servant leaders recognize the deep need people have to celebrate and find ways to make it happen.

Servant leaders celebrate what God has done. "*I will sing to the Lord, for he is highly exalted. The horse and its rider he has hurled into the sea*" (Exodus 15:1-12). Moses' celebration focused on what God had done. He resisted the temptation to say, "Did you see what happened when I stretched out my hand over the water?" He focused on God's work, not his own. *Selfish* leaders celebrate what they have done, *good* leaders celebrate what 'we' have done; *servant* leaders celebrate what God has done!

Servant leaders celebrate what God will do. "*You will lead the people you have redeemed. In your strength you will guide them*" (Exodus 15:13-18). With these words, Moses' song shifts from what God has just done to what He will do. He skillfully uses the time of celebration not only to look back, but to restate the vision of where God is taking them. He reminds the people that there is more in store for them and more victories ahead. Celebrations provide a wonderful opportunity for servant leaders to remind people of the ultimate goal. The celebration of victories provides the encouragement needed to tackle the next challenge or obstacle. Moses likely had no idea about the challenges that he would soon face, but he wisely used this time to build confidence in God's ability to take them to their final destination.

What has God done for you and the group you lead that you can celebrate today or this week? Sing a song…or at least find a way to celebrate!

For further reflection and discussion:

1. Do I lead with celebration or do I consider it a waste of time and resources?

2. Have I created a culture of celebration among those I lead?

3. Do my celebrations focus on my own achievements, those of our team, or on God's work among us?

4. Have I learned to use every celebration to remind people of the vision for our group?

5. What can our group do today or this week to celebrate?

29. MOSES: DEALING WITH DISCONTENT

Three days after the exuberant celebration of victory over Pharaoh's army, Moses faces a huge leadership challenge. *So the people grumbled against Moses, saying, "What are we to drink?"* (Exodus 15:24). A few weeks later, more challenges: *In the desert the whole community grumbled against Moses and Aaron* (Exodus 16:2). A short time later, they again grumble about the lack of water (Exodus17). It was hot, they were tired and hungry, and they expressed their discontentment by grumbling, claiming that Moses and Aaron *brought us out into this desert to starve this entire assembly to death* (Exodus16:3). What can we learn from Moses about how servant leaders respond when followers are discontent?

Servant leaders cry out to God when facing discontent! Moses' first response when people complained was to cry out to God (Exodus 15:25, 17:4). Servant leaders do not lead alone and do not need to depend on their own resources or wisdom to navigate the challenges of leadership. Thank God we have an ever present leadership coach!

Servant leaders anticipate discontent. Moses had already been in the desert for 40 years. He knew that it was a harsh environment and that there would be times of thirst and hunger. Furthermore, he understood that followers typically think primarily of their own needs and desires. When difficulties come, their lack of faith is expressed in grumbling. Moses' followers must have expected to go straight from slavery to a land flowing with milk and honey, but he anticipated a time in the harsh desert.

Servant leaders separate their leadership from the discontent. The crowd clearly directed their complaints at Moses, but he didn't take it personally. As a servant leader Moses recognized that the vision was not his and neither were the complaints! He reminds the people, *You are not grumbling against us, but against the Lord* (Exodus16:8). Leaders need a certain amount of 'self-detachment' from their role and realize that followers may have issues that have nothing to do with their leadership. Certainly there are times when the discontent of followers is a result of our poor leadership. Then we should ask God to reveal that and change our leadership. But in this case, Moses was not at fault. He was able to separate his leadership role from his own identity and was therefore able to react calmly to the complaints of the crowd. He did not defend his position or authority as leaders are tempted to do when attacked. He did get angry at the disobedience of the followers, but he did not seem to direct his anger at their grumbling, just their disobedience to God's instructions (Exodus 16:20).

Servant leaders combat discontent by recasting vision. As soon as God provided water, through Moses He made a new promise to the people (Exodus15:26). After providing manna, He revealed His glory (Exodus16:10). Moses realized that the complaints were not a food and water issue; they were a vision issue.

When people complain about their salary or working conditions, it may well be that they have lost the vision. Servant leaders will not refuse to address the physical needs but seek to turn people's attention back to the vision. They help followers interpret the current situation in light of the end goal and call followers to endure present hardships for the sake of future success.

This discontent, as we will see later in our study, would give birth to direct criticism and finally, open rebellion. But for now, Moses safely navigated the turbulent waters of discontent and gives us hope that we can also make it through.

For further reflection and discussion:

1. Have I cried out to God when facing discontent or do I seek to resolve issues in my own strength?

2. How have I dealt with discontent in my organization?

3. Have I taken it personally or am I able to remain detached from the attacks?

4. In what ways have my followers expressed discontent in the past six months?

5. Are any of their complaints legitimate leadership issues which I need to address?

6. Who can help me know which ones are leadership issues and which are simply issues of discontent?

7. Have I recast the vision for my grumbling followers? Is it clear in my mind that God will take me through the current situation to accomplish His vision?

30. MOSES: LEARNING TO DELEGATE

Lights, camera, action! Picture Moses, his staff in hand, striking a dry rock, and while the elders watch, water gushes out. From there he moves to the battlefield where his extended hands won the victory over the Amalekites. These scenes make Moses look like a great leader getting the job done! But God is preparing him for a major leadership lesson. At the rock, others simply watch. On the battlefield, Moses gets tired and realized that he needed the help of Aaron and Hur to win the battle. But it took a visit from Moses' father-in-law, Jethro, to teach him that servant leaders learn to delegate. *When his father-in-law saw all that Moses was doing for the people, he said, "What is this you are doing for the people? Why do you alone sit as judge, while all these people stand around you from morning till evening?...What you are doing is not good"* (Exodus 18:14, 17).

Jethro, with this rebuke, gives Moses a powerful leadership lesson. In spite of the great accomplishments Moses had achieved, his leadership was *not good* because he was doing it alone. Moses was serving the people by attempting to meet their needs. That's a great servant heart, but poor leadership. Servant leaders recognize that the best way to serve others is to empower them to share in the work. Jethro taught Moses that servant leaders are not successful because of the work they do but the way they empower others to work through delegation. What can we learn about delegation from Jethro and Moses?

Delegation happens intentionally. By default, Moses was working hard like many leaders. People were crowding around him with their needs, and he was busy! Servant leaders make a conscious choice to stop doing the work and deliberately focus on delegating. It will never happen by accident.

Delegation lightens the load. Moses was carrying a huge burden from morning until evening every day. Jethro advised him to share the load with others so that he would be able *to stand the strain* (Exodus 18:23). Moses' leadership would never have lasted for 40 years if he would have continued at the pace he was going. Servant leaders recognize that an integral part of leading is to set a pace that is sustainable and allow others to lighten the load.

Delegation empowers others. As Moses called capable men to assist in the work, these leaders were able to develop their own potential. Nothing is more empowering to an emerging leader than when a seasoned leader looks them in the eye and says, "I believe you can do this!" Selfish leaders delegate to accomplish their own goals, but servant leaders delegate to empower and develop others. They delight in seeing others grow in their leadership capacity.

Delegation accomplishes the task. Jethro wisely concluded that when Moses would delegate the work, *all these people will go home satisfied* (Exodus 18:23). Insecure leaders believe that no one else can do the job as well as they can, so they refuse to delegate. Servant leaders recognize that when work is shared, the task will be completed. These leaders realize they are *responsible* to see that the work is done but not *able* to do it all alone.

To Moses' credit, he listened to the wise counsel of Jethro and made immediate changes in his leadership style. Everyone benefited from his change, and I'm sure his wife and children were excited to see him home for supper that night for the first time in a long time!

For further reflection and discussion:

1. Do I have a "Jethro" in my life?

2. Do I invite them to speak into my leadership practices?

3. Evaluate your leadership with the following questions:

    Am I guilty of trying to do all the work myself?

    Can I sustain my pace of leadership for the long term?

    Have I told anyone lately, "I believe you can do this"? Who was it?

4. Reflect on how Moses chose the men to lead. What qualifications did he consider?

5. What is my plan to develop others around me?

6. Am I consciously looking for things that others can do which will build them up and help accomplish the vision God has for our group?

7. What steps can I take today to delegate?

31. MOSES: LEADING FROM THE PRESENCE

Nothing more profoundly shaped Moses' leadership than the time he spent in God's presence. When Moses came down from Mount Sinai with the two tablets of the Testimony in his hands, he was not aware that his face was radiant because he had spoken with the LORD (Exodus 34:29). This physical transformation was only an external sign of the relationship God desires to have with every servant leader. In what way does being in God's presence make a difference in our leadership?

Leading from God's presence shapes the leader. There is no doubt that Moses' life was deeply molded by his frequent face-to-face encounters with God. His encounter with the burning bush was a one-time event that confirmed his call to lead, but these regular encounters with God made him a great leader. In God's presence, Moses learned to know the awesome God of the burning bush in a relationship so deep that they talked like friends (Exodus 33:11). Moses didn't go into God's presence only for leadership training or instruction; he went to meet his God. He wasn't seeking a supernatural glow on his face to impress the followers, but he was simply transformed by God's presence. Time in God's presence transforms character and shapes the leader's inner person. In God's presence, my own sin, selfishness, or wrong motives are exposed and changed. I find strength to continue on and courage to do what is right.

Leading from God's presence provides direction to the leader. Moses obtained direction from God as he spent time in His presence. He came down from the mountain with the Ten Commandments as well as the blueprint for how God's people should live. Furthermore, Moses led the people to meet God as he had done (Exodus 19:17). Servant leaders experience God's presence and then invite others to join them. They direct people to God's plan, not their own dream or vision.

The cloud of God's presence was a constant indication of God's direction. Moses longed for this direction to the extent that he said to God, *"If your Presence does not go with us, do not send us up from here"* (Exodus 33:15). I long for such clear physical manifestation of God's direction and often forget that Jesus promised each of His followers the guidance of the Spirit of God (Jn. 16:13). Servant leaders find time to get into God's presence for clear direction for themselves and those who follow.

Leading from God's presence demands sacrifice from the leader. There's a cost to being in God's presence. For Moses on the mountain, it was 40 days without food or water! In other seasons of his leadership he found time on a regular basis to enter the 'tent of meeting.' God doesn't charge money for His presence, but there is a price to be paid. We all want the glow on our face, but few want to pay the price of daily spending time with God or seasons of fasting to seek Him!

Servant leaders pay the price for God's presence. They are changed in His presence in ways that transform their leadership at home, in the marketplace, or in church.

Their leadership is no longer about calling people to reach their own goals, but calling people to also experience God's presence and reach His goals. When their leadership flows out of time in God's presence, followers will see the radiance of God in their lives.

For further reflection and discussion:

1. Can my followers tell today that I've been with Jesus?

2. Is my leadership focused primarily on getting people to reach my goals or helping people reach God's goals for our organization?

3. What difference would it make in my leadership if each day began with a time in God's presence?

4. Is my time in the 'tent of meeting' an integral part of my leadership or simply another task on my 'to do' list?

5. Do I spend enough time in God's presence to know His direction for the decisions I need to make today?

32. MOSES: FACE-DOWN LEADERSHIP

Servant leaders recognize that they stand in the gap between God and those they lead. In the last chapter, we observed that Moses led by being in God's presence. A significant part of his time in God's presence was spent on his face interceding on behalf of the people. *The next day Moses said to the people, "You have committed a great sin. But now I will go up to the LORD; perhaps I can make atonement for your sin"* (Exodus 32:30). His face-down leadership has much to teach us as servant leaders.

Face-down leadership focuses on the needs of others. Servant leaders petition God for the needs of their people. *So Moses went back to the LORD and said, "Oh, what a great sin these people have committed! They have made themselves gods of gold"* (Exodus 32:31). It is natural to ask God to meet our own needs, and there is certainly a time for this, but servant leaders focus on the needs of others. In face-down leadership we serve those we lead by bringing their needs to God in prayer.

Face-down leadership requires sacrifice. Like so much of servant leadership, intercession is costly. For

Moses, it meant that time after time he returned to God to bring the needs of the people. He sacrificed his time and mental and emotional energy on behalf of those he was serving. He was even willing to sacrifice his own position with God for the sake of others! *"But now, please forgive their sin-- but if not, then blot me out of the book you have written"* (Exodus 32:32). As they intercede, servant leaders sacrifice their own needs for the sake of their followers.

Face-down leadership releases the burden of leadership. Moses acknowledged that the people he was leading were really God's people when he told God, *"Remember that this nation is your people"* (Exodus 33:13). Moses felt the weight of leading an entire nation and knew that God had called him to that role, but prayer allowed him to gain the perspective that these were not "his" people. He was responsible *to* the people, but not *for* the people. Servant leaders release leadership burdens through intercession. The church, business, or group that you lead is not really 'your' group; they are simply God's people whom He has entrusted to your leadership. We are not at the top of the leadership chart; we simply act as stewards of God's people. It is easy to lose this focus unless we spend time on our face in prayer. Servant leaders find the balance between active intercession and conscious release of burdens.

Face-down leadership touches the heart of God. *And the LORD said to Moses, "I will do the very thing you have asked, because I am pleased with you and I know you by name"* (Exodus 33:17). I am amazed at how Moses' intercession touches God's heart and changes outcomes. God saw that the heart of Moses was not selfish but focused on others. Moses' requests reminded God of His own promises and character. Repeatedly, God acted in response to Moses' prayers. If you want to touch God's heart, practice face-down leadership focused on the needs of others! Whether you are called to lead in church, education, business, or the arts, touch God's heart by falling on your face to intercede for those you lead.

For further reflection and discussion:

1. What percent of my time in prayer focuses on my needs? How much is centered on the needs of others?

2. Are my prayers primarily concerned with the success of my own organization or God's glory?

3. Do I recognize that I am in the gap between 'my' people and God, or do I see myself as the leader on top?

4. Do I have a plan for how I will pray for those under my leadership?

33. MOSES: SERVING THE TEAM

Moses led the people out of Egypt, received God's commandments on the mountain, and was now ready for action! The first matter needing attention was to build a tabernacle, a place of worship for the new nation. Moses had learned from Jethro that he could not do all the work alone and this time doesn't even try! He immediately calls others to help and models for all servant leaders six steps to build an effective team.

Select the right members. (Exodus 35:30-35) Moses chose two persons, Bezalel and Oholiab, to lead the team that would construct the tabernacle. Finding the right persons is critical to the success of a team, and servant leaders would do well to use the same criteria that Moses used. First, he recognized their *character*. Bezalel was filled with the Spirit of God. Secondly, he chose men with skill, ability, and knowledge. Servant leaders look for and expect *competence* on their team. Finally, he chose men who could teach others. This reflected their leadership *capacity*. He needed more than workers; he needed leaders.

It is instructive to consider what criteria Moses did <u>not</u> use. He did not choose based on family relationships or tribal affiliation. He did not choose based on demonstrated loyalty to his leadership or give positions as a reward. Servant leaders keep their selection process focused on the right issues: character, competence, and capacity.

Recognize them publically. (Exodus 35:30) Moses introduced the team to the nation. Servant leaders ensure that everyone knows what is happening. The team needs to know their responsibilities and accountability, but the larger group also needs to understand the work of the team.

Give them the needed resources. (Exodus 36:3) *They received from Moses all the offerings.* Moses provided the team with the physical resources they needed. Servant leaders anticipate the needs of the team and ensure that they have what is required for success. This may be physical needs or it may be less tangible needs such as further training or encouragement.

Help them solve problems. (Exodus 36:3-7) Soon after the work began, the team encountered a rather unusual problem: the people were bringing too many gifts! Moses dealt with it immediately because it was an issue that caused the work to stop. Servant leaders don't interfere with the work, but serve their team by recognizing when obstacles need to be removed. They act quickly to release the team to continue working. As soon as this issue was resolved, the team continued working and produced incredible results that take four chapters to report (Exodus 36:8 -39:31).

Inspect their work. (Exodus 39:43) Moses recognized that delegation and encouragement do not negate the need for inspection. He released them to do the job and didn't interfere with the process. But servant leaders hold followers to a high level of accountability and expect results from their teams. They do not look *critically* but they do look *carefully.*

Bless their accomplishments. (Exodus 39:43) *Moses blessed them.* Three simple but profound words describe Moses' final act with this team. Servant leaders find ways to bless their teams. It may be a simple word of encouragement, public affirmation, a financial reward, time with the leader, greater opportunities for service, or other ways. Servant leaders don't call attention to their own accomplishments, but bless the teams who work with them.

For further reflection and discussion:

1. Do I have the right people on my team(s)?

2. What criteria do I use to select team members?

3. How do I assess the character of my team members?

4. In my context, what wrong criteria for choosing team members are common?

5. Do I 'inspect' the work of my team in ways that clearly call them to accountability?

6. How have I (or how should I) publically recognized the role and responsibility of my team?

7. What are the resources my team requires?

8. Have I done all I can to ensure that they have these resources?

9. What problems does my team face?

10. Which problems should be mine to handle and which ones should I encourage them to solve on their own?

11. Have I acted quickly to remove obstacles for my team to do their work?

12. Do I inspect the work of my team often enough? Too often?

13. Do they know clearly what I am looking for and what I expect?

14. In what ways can I bless my team?

15. What will motivate them towards continued service?

34. MOSES: SERVING THOSE WHO WON'T FOLLOW

The grumbling of the people right after the Red Sea crossing soon turned vicious. First, the 'sister who brought him out of the water as an infant and his brother complained about his wife. Then, after the spies brought back their negative report, the entire community grumbled and threatened to choose a new leader who would take them back to Egypt. Finally, Korah led an attempted coup with 250 key leaders. And you thought your people were difficult? Moses' response to these attacks helps us understand how servant leaders respond to those who simply won't follow.

Servant leaders let God fight for them. The attacks were vicious and brutal. The first one attacked his wife and called his authority into question. Korah's rebellion was an outright attempt to take over his leadership. The response of Moses to each of these attacks was remarkable. He didn't defend himself! Self-defense is an instinctive response. Nothing takes more strength than not fighting back! Leaders who are not servants react defensively when followers don't follow. They use power or manipulation to force and control. Servant leaders don't have that agenda. They allow God to fight for them. This requires deep brokenness in the face of personal attacks. It is no coincidence that it is in the context of Miriam and Aaron's attack that the Bible tells us, *Now Moses was a very humble man, more humble than anyone else on the face of the earth* (Numbers 12:3). Staying humble in the face of an attack is difficult, and Moses, while a great example, did get very angry when Dathan and Abiram refused to come after he called for them (Numbers 16:12-15). Servant leaders surrender their own ego for the sake of God's agenda for the organization. They wait for God to vindicate their leadership role.

Servant leaders extend grace to rebels. Amazingly, after Moses refuses to defend himself and God vindicates his authority to lead, he intercedes for them! Moses cried out to the Lord after Miriam was stricken with leprosy. When the people rebelled, Moses and Aaron immediately fell on their faces and pleaded with God for mercy. Likewise, in Korah's rebellion, they also interceded with God on behalf of the nation. Even after the earth opened and swallowed the rebels, Moses and Aaron interceded during the plague that killed 14,700 people. I'm afraid I would be thinking, *Go get them God!* Servant leaders keep serving others, and at this point, rebels need an intercessor, not a judge.

Servant leaders continue leading with truth. When things finally quiet down after Korah's death, the people realize their mistake but start heading in the wrong direction again (Numbers 14:40-45). Without a hint of a vengeful spirit, Moses calmly reminds the people of the direction they should go and warns them of what will happen if they refuse. Our natural instinct would be to let them go and suffer, but servant leaders are committed to lead, even when people don't want to follow! Back at the burning bush Moses was called to lead, and his willingness to serve in this role didn't change with every obstacle. He was still committed to pointing out the direction God was calling them to go. Servant leaders don't quit easily! Leadership is not about them, their vision, or their agenda. Rather, they seek to be faithful to God's call on them to keep leading, and even in the face of sluggish followers, they remain strong leaders.

When you find yourself in a situation where, like Moses, you are doing your best but followers don't want to follow, ask God for the grace to serve like Moses.

For further reflection and discussion:

1. When is the last time I felt that followers challenged my leadership?

    What was my response?

    What was happening in my heart at the time?

2. Am I humble enough to resist my own desire for revenge when I'm attacked?

3. What would it take for God to break my pride?

4. Are there times that I become angry at those I lead? What does it indicate?

5. When those who follow me go against my advice, can I still earnestly pray for them? Why or why not?

6. When I feel resistance to my leadership, am I able to continue providing strong leadership with a good heart or do I withdraw and allow a leadership vacuum?

7. What is the result and in what way is God inviting me to change?

35. MOSES: A SINNING SERVANT

Moses is a great example of a servant leader, but he wasn't perfect! Numbers 20 records the story of the sin that would keep Moses out of the Promised Land. The people are thirsty and blame Moses again. Moses cries out to God for direction, and God instructs him to speak to the rock and promises that water would come out. Instead Moses spoke to the people in anger, *"Listen, you rebels, must we bring water out of this rock?"* Then he struck the rock twice and water came out. God immediately told him and Aaron that because of their sin they would not enter the land of promise. In a moment of anger, forty years of faithful leadership seems to disappear! Still, we can learn lessons from his failure. What he did *not do* goes against every natural response and serves as an example to all of us of how servant leaders deal with sin.

Moses did not blame the people. The most natural response when I sin is to find someone else to blame! Certainly Moses had some legitimate reasons to blame the people, and all of us can sympathize with the way he called them rebels! They had again opposed his leadership and quarreled with him and Aaron. Most of us would have lost our temper and promptly blamed the people. But Moses recognized that the pressure of the moment simply revealed the sin in his heart. Servant leaders continually cry out to God for Him to deal with their hearts and refuse to blame family members, co-workers, associates, or followers for what they do in times of pressure.

Moses did not blame God. Moses had just mourned the death of his sister, Miriam, and after this experience at the rock very quickly said farewell to his closest associate, Aaron. It was a rough month to lead, and I would find it easy to accuse God of overreacting! Moses could have argued that he had been blameless for years and surely one mistake wasn't as serious as God judged it. But again, Moses demonstrates his brokenness and humility as he does not blame God for his judgment. I don't find any record of Moses pleading with God to reverse His judgment; instead he humbly accepts what has happened. Moses, like all servant leaders, recognized that God was more interested in the condition of his heart than about his leadership credentials.

Moses did not cover up his sin. When I sin, I quickly move to minimize the damage and ensure that as few as possible know about it. But Moses wrote the story just as it happened and we are still reading about it thousands of years later! His sin in this case was public as leaders sins' often are. But there are other times when leaders' sin is private and unknown to those they lead. One temptation all leaders face is to pretend in public to be better than we actually are in private. Servant leaders appropriately acknowledge both their sin and God's gracious forgiveness.

Moses did not stop leading. The final months of Moses leadership must have been incredibly difficult. Why not just step down? Yes, there are times when leaders sin and need to step down from their position. But most of the time God simply asks us to continue leading. Our enemy whispers that we are not worthy to continue, but God's grace gives us strength to continue. Servant leaders who deal with their sin like Moses drink more deeply from God's grace and more freely extend it to those they lead.

What a difference it would make in our world if we were leaders with a servant heart who respond to sin like Moses. Can we respond without defensiveness and blame, allowing God to expose and purify our hearts, then continuing to serve those we lead with an even greater sense of God's grace as long as He allows us to guide them?

For further reflection and discussion:

1. What typically happens to me when I am under intense pressure in my leadership? Do I get angry, abusive, withdrawn, or bitter?

   What does this reveal about my heart?

2. The last time I sinned, who was I tempted to blame?

3. Are there times I have blamed God for my sin? What has been the result and what needs to change?

4. How do I try to cover my sin?

   What has been the result of this?

5. What is the right balance between being open about my sin and wisely not disclosing too many details to others?

6. How does David's observation in Ps. 32:5 provide instruction to all leaders about dealing with sin?

7. Are there secret sins in my life that have the potential to sabotage my leadership?

8. What is God calling me to do about them? (Reflect on 1 Timothy 5:24 and 1 Corinthians 10:12)

36. MOSES: LEADING IN-BETWEEN

We've looked at Moses' leadership from many different perspectives as he led through some victories and also tough times. But hidden in the chapters of specific incidents about which we read I find the greatest challenge Moses faced: leading in-between. Think about it. For forty years Moses led the nation of Israel around and around in the desert waiting for everyone from that generation to die. They had left the past behind, but the dream of the future was still a distant goal. It was leadership going nowhere except to funerals! By the most conservative estimates, one million people died during those 40 years. That's about 68 funerals a day! I like baptisms, child dedications, new members' classes, weddings, sales parties, etc. They are signs of growth and moving forward. But what leader likes funerals or leading when the goal is far in the future?

While Moses' situation was extremely unusual, there may be times when we are called to lead when the way forward is not clear or the usual marks of progress are not available. It was not Moses' fault that they would not reach the Promised Land and it was not a result of poor leadership. When we find ourselves in that desert experience what can we learn from Moses about how servant leaders deal with these periods?

Surrender your own dreams. When he began leading, Moses at least had something to look forward to accomplish: he was going to lead a nation into a new land. That's enough to get any leader's adrenaline moving! Moses anticipated a couple months journey through the desert. Instead, he got forty years of in-between leadership. To keep leading, Moses had to surrender his own dreams of grand success. There are no awards, no prizes, and no coveted speaking engagements for those who lead in the desert. Desert leadership is not fun! Moses could not have lead in this desert before he first had his own desert- training. Death to self is required before anyone can do this and only servant leaders are willing to sign up for these jobs!

Keep people moving. For forty years, Moses kept people moving. Some of it was practical; they had to find new places for water and graves! But I think Moses also realized that even in the desert places of life, people need direction, and they need leaders that motivate them to keep moving. I would be tempted to find a shade tree and wait for the next generation! But Moses, day after day, sounded the call to pack up and move on.

Focus on the eternal. What kept Moses going all these years? Certainly it wasn't the direction they were going or the desire to achieve great things. It wasn't the hope of a promotion or increased salary. As I reflect on what kept him going, I conclude that when all the external things leaders look for were stripped away, Moses was left with the most important: his relationship with the One who called him. He was able to look past the funerals, past the complaints, and past the sand in his tent, and keep eternity in perspective.

He was looking ahead to his reward (Hebrews

11:26). His focus on the eternal allowed him to persevere through the desert and remain effective as a leader.

As I reflect on Moses' leadership in the desert, I want to honor those among us whom God has called to lead in places that may seem to not have the recognition and honor of coveted leadership positions. I salute those who work behind the scenes, those who are serving daily to make someone else's dream come true, those who are called to lead others through a transition and then fade into the background, the interim pastors and small business owners. May God put your names close to Moses' in His hall of fame!

For further reflection and discussion:

1. In what way is my present leadership 'in-between' the past and the future?

2. What are the things to which I must die to be able to lead people through a time with no visible progress?

3. How can I motivate people to keep moving, when the ultimate goal seems out of reach?

4. What can I do today that will help me focus on the eternal rather than my current situation?

37. MOSES: THE GREAT COMMUNICATOR

In the fortieth year, on the first day of the eleventh month, Moses proclaimed to the Israelites all that the LORD had commanded him concerning them (Deuteronomy 1:3).

After 40 years of leading the people in the wilderness, Moses nears the end of his leadership journey. Because of his sin, he will not be allowed to enter the Promised Land. Before he breathes his last, God has two more tasks for him to accomplish. The first is to communicate to the new generation God's direction for their lives. As a young man, Moses was *"powerful in speech"* (Acts 7:22); but now as a seasoned leader, Moses is a great communicator. The verse above sets the stage for the entire book of Deuteronomy in which Moses makes his final address to the people. How does he communicate as a servant leader?

He represents. Moses now recognized that he was not the primary communicator. He was simply representing God to the people and proclaimed all that the LORD had commanded. This is a key difference between servant leaders and selfish leaders. Servant leaders recognize that as they communicate, they represent the voice of God. Representing God in our communication makes a profound difference in the tone, content, and motive of our speech, whether this is in a board room, staff meeting, public address, or casual conversation. Jesus represented the Father as He spoke and recognized that what He said and how He said it was directed by God (John 12:49). I am more aware of this when I stand before people in public, but I believe it is God's intention for me in every conversation.

He repeats. The book of Deuteronomy is a repetition of the law of God. Although it seems monotonous at times, Moses realized that people tend to forget and leaders need to remind them. In his case, he was also dealing with a new generation of people and wanted to ensure that they were fully aware of all that God wanted them to know. Servant leaders repeat vision, direction, and instruction to keep followers focused on common goals (See 2 Peter 1:12).

He reveals. A quick reading of the book of Deuteronomy reveals that Moses masterfully paints a picture of the future for the people of Israel. He recounts past victories as an assurance of a great future. He talks about the land flowing with 'milk and honey.' Again and again he promises them God's blessing for obedience. Great communicators paint vivid pictures of the future that keep people focused on their objectives. Some leaders use words to manipulate people to their own selfish ends but servant leaders paint pictures to motivate followers to fulfill God's plan for their lives.

He rebukes. Moses' communication to the people often contained a warning of the consequences of disobedience. Revealing a positive future comes naturally to many leaders. But Moses realized that servant leaders communicate not only what people want to hear, but what they need to hear. Forty years of wandering in the desert made Moses very aware of the price of sin and he doesn't dilute the message! His words in Deuteronomy 8:11 are typical, *Be careful that you do not forget the LORD your God, failing to observe his command, his laws and his decrees that I am giving you this day.* Servant leaders are not afraid to warn people of the consequences of wrong actions.

Servant leaders learn from Moses to rely not on their own ability to persuade but to communicate God's words to the people they lead.

For further reflection and discussion:

1. Does my speech reflect God's intention for those who hear me?

2. Am I continually aware of my role to represent God to those who follow me? What can I do to grow in this awareness?

3. Do I repeat the vision often enough? Too often?

4. Do I consistently paint a picture for my followers of where we are going?

    Is it done in a way that inspires a shared vision of the future?

5. What creative ways can I use to keep this in front of people?

6. Am I willing to be honest with people about the price of disobedience?

    Can I do this with pure motives?

38. MOSES: LEAVING A LEGACY

Then Moses went out and spoke these words to all Israel: "I am now a hundred and twenty years old and I am no longer able to lead you. The LORD has said to me, 'You shall not cross the Jordan.' The LORD your God himself will cross over ahead of you. He will destroy these nations before you, and you will take possession of their land. Joshua also will cross over ahead of you, as the LORD said" (Deuteronomy 31:1-3).

One final task remained for Moses' leadership, passing the baton to the next leader, Joshua. This transition left a legacy for the children of Israel and shows us the way servant leaders handle similar transitions.

Servant leaders step down. Moses was very old by our standards and told the people that he is no longer able to lead. However, he was not quitting because of his age. Scripture is clear that his eyes were not weak nor his strength gone (Deuteronomy 34:7). Moses was still able and ready to cross over the river and see his dreams come true. But it was time for him to step down. Why? *The LORD has said to me...* We all love the call to positions, but find it very difficult to hear God calling us from positions. Moses was a servant and realized that leadership was a gift from God that could be revoked at any time. God may tell us to step down at the height of success, or when we grow old. In either case, servant leaders don't cling to their positions and find the right time to step down.

Servant leaders lift up. Woven throughout the story of Moses' leadership is his relationship with and training of Joshua, preparing him for leadership. His action at the end of his life was not a hasty decision; he had been training Joshua for years! He gave Joshua responsibilities like standing watch at the tent of meeting, spying out the land and fighting the Amalekites. He helped prepare Joshua for leadership many times by simply taking him along with him as he demonstrated leadership. They were together on the mountain when God gave Moses the law. Servant leaders realize that they will not be in a position forever and that God has called them to lift up other leaders.

Servant leaders hand off. Moses didn't simply get out of the way; he deliberately installed Joshua as the new leader. In a powerful symbolic act, Moses laid his hands on Joshua in public and released him to lead (Numbers 27:18-22). He took the initiative to ensure that his successor was properly trained and then released to do the work. It was a beautiful example of a smooth transfer of power. Many leaders stumble at this point either by not being willing to release the work to someone else or by not declaring publicly their confidence in the new leaders' ability. Servant leaders bless their successors and then get out of the way. They leave a legacy as they release the baton into the hands of their trained successor. They finish well!

Moses, what a leader! For the past several chapters, we've examined his leadership. He was certainly not perfect but was an outstanding example of a person who learned to lead others with the heart of a servant. We do well to learn from his life, his victories and struggles as we lead others in the way of Jesus.

For further reflection and discussion:

1. What have I observed in leaders who are not willing to step down?

   What happens to them and to those who follow?

2. If God asked me today to relinquish my role, would I willingly obey?

3. Am I actively training others to take over my responsibilities?

4. Have I identified someone who can take over my role?

5. Do I purposefully take an apprentice with me for on the job training?

6. When it is time for my transition, what will I do publically to pass on the baton to others?

7. What key things have I learned from this study of the life of Moses and what steps do I need to take to put them into practice?

39. QUALITY ASSURANCE: ABOVE REPROACH

Every manufacturing business is concerned with the quality of their product because they recognize that substandard products will hurt their reputation and ultimately destroy their business. So they invest large amounts of time and money in quality assurance programs to protect their profit. Christian leaders should be even more concerned about assuring the quality of those who lead. We represent God Himself in our business, church, school and home. Paul, in his letter to Timothy, a young servant leader, provides a checklist of qualities which are expected in each of our lives. He writes specifically to those called to be overseers in 1 Timothy 3:1-7 but the standards are useful for each of us in whatever place we exercise our leadership. In the next chapters we'll examine one quality from Paul's list and find a biblical leader whose life illustrates this quality.

Before Paul goes into specifics, he begins his list with this general characteristic, *"Now the overseer must be above reproach."* (NIV) We don't often use the word reproach in modern speech. To live above reproach means to be above suspicion, blameless, and having clean hands. Let's examine these more closely to understand what it looks like for a servant leader to live above reproach.

Living above reproach means to be above suspicion. Leaders live in the open. Their lives are seen by many others who can quickly come to wrong conclusions about the action and motives of a leader. Some leaders do little to avoid suspicion and care little about whether or not their actions seem questionable. Suspicion is unsubstantiated but still drains trust from the relationship between the leader and follower. So a servant leader goes the second mile to avoid even the "appearance of evil" (1 Thessalonians 5:22, KJV). The servant leader is concerned not only with whether or not one is technically guilty, but whether or not the action produces suspicion in the lives of those who follow.

Living above reproach means to be blameless. When things go wrong, our human nature looks for someone to blame and the leader is often the target of this blame. Sometimes the charges are true and the leader is at fault. Paul calls us to a higher standard as servant leaders as he challenges us to be blameless. This does not mean perfection or no one would measure up. Servant leaders take responsibility for their mistakes and seek forgiveness when needed. But in addition, they live in such a way that their character and lives of integrity are blameless. Accusations made against them are so far from the truth that they don't stick. Their leadership does not attract blame.

Living above reproach means to have clean hands. Clean hands symbolize innocence. Blame and suspicion can be present even if no wrong has been done; clean hands indicate that no wrong has happened. Paul calls servant leaders to possess hands that are clean and bring no reproach to the One they serve.

Daniel was a biblical leader who was above reproach. His enemies tried to find fault with him but could not. They tried to accuse him but he was blameless. His hands were clean. He passed the quality assurance checklist as a leader above reproach and provides a model for each of us to follow. Take a moment to ask yourself if your leadership is above reproach.

For further reflection and discussion:

1. Am I content to be simply "not guilty" or do I strive to be above suspicion?

2. Are there ways that I lead which give ground for others to suspect that something is not right in my life?

3. How is God calling me to change?

4. When I have been blamed for issues that happened under my leadership, were there elements of truth in the accusations?

5. If so, how did that affect my ability to represent Christ?

6. When I have made mistakes, have I taken responsibility to admit them and make things right as far as possible with me?

7. Can I honestly say that my hands are clean? Are there areas of my life that no one even suspects but which I know to be unclean? What is God inviting me to do in response?

40. QUALITY ASSURANCE: HUSBAND OF ONE WIFE

After the general quality "above reproach" Paul quickly focuses his checklist on an area that deeply impacts all servant leaders who are called to be, "the husband of but one wife" (1 Timothy 3:2). At first glance most of us who are married would go ahead and mark this requirement as complete. Those who are single easily read on to the next item on the list. Women assume this is irrelevant. But let's dig a bit deeper. Paul is certainly calling leaders to avoid polygamy, but this quality assurance means far more than possessing a single marriage certificate. Further, his instruction does not limit leadership to those who are married or he would disqualify himself. Instead Paul is calling all leaders to honor God's standards of marriage and purity. How can we practice this?

Leaders of purity honor covenants. Marriage is a covenant relationship, a binding agreement between two parties accompanied by solemn vows. Many leaders seek to separate their personal relationship with their spouse from their leadership. They argue that what happens at home has no impact on their leadership. Servant leaders recognize that honoring their promises reflects strong character which begins with the marriage covenant.

It was common in Paul's day for men to have several wives (polygamy) or successive wives (divorce and remarriage). Both violate the covenant plan of God. Paul asserts that God's plan is for one man and one woman to remain together for life and calls leaders to honor that standard. He calls men to be a "one woman man."

Honoring the marriage covenant goes beyond simply remaining together. Some remain married but have long ago left their spouse emotionally. Servant leaders honor other parts of that covenant such as "to love and cherish" the other. They refuse to allow careers, ministry, sports or hobbies to keep them from building a solid relationship with their spouse.

Single leaders honor the covenant of marriage by living lives of purity and supporting those who are married with prayer and encouragement. In return servant leaders who are married affirm God's call to those who are single and encourage their walk of purity.

Leaders of purity honor morality. Paul was writing in the context of a culture where immorality was accepted as normal. His call is for leaders to remain sexually pure both in thought and deed. Servant leaders carefully guard their eyes and thoughts in this area. They seek accountability from other godly leaders to help them in this area realizing that all will be tempted to compromise and many have fallen in this area.

Leaders of purity honor relationships. Finally, Paul's challenge is for each of us to examine the way we relate to members of the opposite sex. It is not enough to remain married to one person; it also matters how we relate to others at our place of work, in the market place, in church and in social settings. Because of their commitment to be a "one woman man" servant leaders are diligent to create boundaries that guard relationships with the opposite sex so that they avoid even the appearance of evil.

Boaz was a biblical leader who modeled what it means to be a "one woman man." He waited patiently for God's timing for marriage. He showed honor to Ruth when she gleaned in his field and protected her from the advances of other men with no thought of marriage at that point. Later, he followed the path of honor as he took Ruth to be his wife. Together they became the great grandparents of King David. Boaz passed the quality assurance checklist as "the husband of but one wife" and provides a model for each of us to follow. Take a moment to ask yourself if you are a 'one woman man' or a 'one man woman' by reflecting on the questions below.

For further reflection and discussion:

1. Is the way I relate to my spouse a reflection of God's intent for marriage?

2. If I am not married, have I recognized the implications of God's plan for covenant relationships and am I living in a way that honors that plan?

3. Have I allowed other good things to come before my covenant relationship with my spouse?

   What needs to change?

4. Do I have clear boundaries for the way I relate to members of the opposite sex?

   If so, what are they? If not, what should they be?

5. Have I recently been in any situations which could have led to compromise or the appearance of wrong doing in relationships with the opposite sex?

6. Am I walking in relationship with others who can hold me accountable?

7. In what ways do I need the grace and forgiveness of God in this area?

8. If I have been strong am I tempted to be judgmental of those who are weak?

41. QUALITY ASSURANCE: TEMPERATE

After calling leaders to be blameless and to honor marriage commitments, Paul adds to his quality assurance list; the leader must be *"temperate"* (1 Timothy 3:2). My first response is "What?" Temperate is not a word I use often! Other translations use "vigilant" and "sober-minded." The main idea is the ability to think clearly, especially in contrast to having one's mind clouded by the influence of wine. So how can we lead with clear thinking as temperate or sober-minded servant leaders?

Sober-minded leadership requires clarity. Persons who drink alcohol and drive may be charged with "driving under the influence." Their mind is not clear enough to make good, quick decisions. Paul would say that servant leaders should avoid "leading under the influence." They should keep their minds clear of things which would distract them from their mission. This requires discipline and persistent exercise. Servant leaders discipline their minds to focus on their calling. They are careful about the mental diet they consume. We live in an information age with all sorts of information readily available to us. Effective leaders carefully monitor what they see, hear, and read. They focus on things which are good and right and avoid mental "alcohol" (See Philippians 4:8). Servant leaders also recognize the need to keep their minds strong and find ways to exercise their mind. They keep their minds strong by discussing thoughts and ideas with others, not simply comments about the weather and sports. They read and find time to reflect on what they are learning. They persistently seek to keep their minds clear.

Sober-minded leadership requires perspective. The idea behind the role of an overseer to which Paul refers is one who "sees over." Leaders see things that others do not see. They look behind to learn from the past. They look around to observe current events; they look ahead to anticipate future challenges. Like a person who looks out of the window of an airplane and is able to see in all directions, leaders see from a higher perspective. For some, this perspective comes naturally; other leaders must work hard to develop perspective. They find mentors who can help them see beyond their current realities and discipline themselves to look ahead, behind and around.

Sober-minded leadership requires wisdom. Leaders who are thinking clearly and with temperance are able not only to focus and see the larger picture; but also to understand what should be done as a result. Wisdom is the ability to know what should be done and is strengthened with sober-minded thinking. All leaders are action-oriented and often quickly identify solutions. But servant leaders think soberly about the situation and ask God for the wisdom needed before moving. They balance decisiveness with wisdom.

In scripture, we learn of a group of men who demonstrate this quality, the men of Issachar. They are mentioned among the fighting men of David as, *"Men of*

Issachar, who understood the times and knew what Israel should do-- 200 chiefs, with all their relatives under their command" (1Chronicles 12:32). This group of men had the ability to see what was going on around them, correctly interpret the meaning of these events, and know how to act on this information. Around them were many others who had battle skills, courage, and experience. But these men possessed the extra quality of clear thinking. They were sober-minded leaders and call us to do the same.

For further reflection and discussion:

1. What am I doing to keep my mind focused and strong?

2. What do I typically discuss with others, ideas or events?

3. What good books have I read that stimulate my thinking?

4. How can I develop a larger perspective in my leadership?

5. Is there someone I can talk with who will help me see things I am not seeing?

6. Have I taken time to reflect and look at the bigger picture or am I focused only on the daily tasks?

7. Would my colleagues describe my leadership as wise? Why or why not?

8. Do I naturally tend to move too quickly or too slowly? How can I learn wisdom in my leadership?

42. QUALITY ASSURANCE: SELF-CONTROL

"Now the overseer must be above reproach, the husband of but one wife, temperate, self-controlled, respectable, hospitable, able to teach..." (1 Timothy 3:2).

The fourth quality Paul lists as essential for those who desire to lead like Christ is "self-controlled." He recognized that before seeking to exert influence over others, the leader must be able to exercise self-control. Self-control will be expressed in the life of a servant leader in three key areas.

Servant leaders control their time. Leaders have the same amount of time as everyone else, but they learn to manage their time well. Servant leaders recognize that time is a gift from God, given to allow them to accomplish His purposes for their lives. Therefore they are passionate about using their time in His way. They are diligent to prioritize and work efficiently. But they acknowledge that God wants more than achievement. They balance time for doing and time for being. They invest time in building strong relationships as well as completing tasks. They honor God's plan for Sabbath rest even when the demands of work and family are high.

They take time for personal growth and development to better fulfill God's purposes for their lives and leadership.

Servant leaders control their tongue. Effective leaders understand the words of Solomon, *"The tongue has the power of life and death"* (Proverbs 18:21). In public and private, the words of a leader impact many either for good or bad. Servant leaders have a genuine desire to bless others and make a positive impact in their lives. Therefore, they work diligently to eliminate all lies, gossip, idle talk, slander, and harsh instructions from their tongue. They value relationships but strive to follow Paul's instruction to *"speak the truth in love"* (Ephesians 4:15). They honor confidential information and resist the temptation to exaggerate. They honor their spoken commitments above the law.

Servant leaders control their temper. Leaders have the same emotions as followers. Servant leaders acknowledge and appropriately express their emotions, but recognize that if their emotions are not predictable, people will find it difficult to trust their leadership. Anger is one of the first emotions to be expressed, and leaders are often in situations where they are blamed or attacked. Servant leaders learn that words spoken in anger and decisions made in an angry moment quickly undermine their ability to lead like Jesus.

The term "self-control" may imply that these things can be done with enough willpower. While servant leaders strive to evidence self-control, this character trait is not something we manufacture with our own effort. Servant leaders do not need another 'self-help' book urging them to try harder to be good. Paul notes that self-control is one of the evidences of the Spirit's work in our lives (Galatians 5:23). Servant leaders yield control to the work of the Spirit in their lives and enjoy the fruit of self-control.

Too often self-control is noted when it is absent and flaws are exposed. Samson was a leader who failed in this area. He was called, gifted, and filled with God's Spirit. But he repeatedly acted impulsively and allowed his passions to control his actions rather than exercising self-control. This sabotaged his leadership potential, and his leadership is a tragic example of why Paul calls us to be self-controlled.

For further reflection and discussion:

Take a few moments to reflect on your own life. In which of the three areas mentioned in this issue (time, tongue, temper) do you most need God's help? Work through the questions below for the one you identify.

1. **Time.** Reflect on these scriptures as you respond to the following questions: Ps. 90:12; Eph. 5:15-16 (KJV); Acts 21:5; Exodus 20:8-11; Mark 6:31. How well do I use time to accomplish God's plan for my life?

   Do I get adequate rest for my body?

   Do I spend too much or too little time on building relationships?

   What is my plan for honoring the principle of Sabbath rest?

2. **Tongue.** Read Eph. 4:29. What areas of 'unwholesome talk' come out of my mouth? Which ones are most damaging to my relationships?

What is the root attitude in my heart that leads to sin with my tongue?

What percentage of my talk builds others up and what can I do to improve?

As a leader how can I encourage a culture of speaking 'truth in love' among my followers?

Is there a commitment I have made recently which I have not honored?

3. **Temper.** Read James 1:19-20 and Prov. 29:22. Reflect on the most recent time you became angry. How did you express it and what was the impact of your actions on others?

Do you need to ask forgiveness from those toward whom you have been angry? If so, when will you ask?

43. QUALITY ASSURANCE: RESPECTABLE

Paul's next instruction to Timothy is to find leaders who are *"respectable"* (1Timothy 3:2). Being respectable is much deeper than looking good on the outside or impressing people with charisma or leadership skills. Paul recognized that followers will not follow a leader they do not genuinely respect for long. He understood that positions are given, but respect is earned. He wanted to assure that the leaders who served on his team had earned the respect of those who followed. With this instruction, Paul calls each of us to live as servant leaders earning respect in at least three ways.

Servant leaders are respectable when their lives are principled. Principles, not convenience or public opinion, are the compass for leaders whose lives are respectable. Far too many leaders try to find out what people want; then take their stand based on what is most popular. That may win votes but it will never win respect. Servant leaders base their lives on unchanging principles. They are charitable to those who disagree with their positions but refuse to be swayed by popular opinion. They refuse to lie even in the smallest matter.

They don't exaggerate their reports. They do not compromise what they believe to make more profit or bring another member to their church or another worker in their organization.

Servant leaders are respectable when their lives are selfless. Leaders who are worthy of respect put the needs of others above themselves. Day after day, they lay down their own wishes and surrender their rights to serve others. They focus on others, not themselves. This is not a gimmick to win favor, but a genuine heart attitude of love for others and a commitment to give as leaders rather than to receive. Leaders who serve only themselves may get a lot done and may appear to be successful. They believe that they will be respected because of their position and achievements. But until they focus on others their lives are not worthy of respect. Servant leaders use their positions to serve others, not themselves, and as they do so they earn the right to be respected.

Servant leaders are respectable when their lives are consistent. Respect is earned as a result of consistent behavior over a long period of time. Servant leaders are not seeking instant success or popularity. They begin with the end in mind and focus on long-term results rather than short-term gains. They recognize that a moment of indiscretion can ruin years of consistency, so they guard their lives against secret sins that will eventually surface and destroy their respectability. They are willing to consistently model the way day after day, year after year.

Joseph, the husband of Mary, provides a biblical example of a respectable man. He is described as a *"just"* or *"righteous"* man (Matthew 1:19). When faced with what seemed like an obvious sin in Mary, he determined to act in accordance with his principles and also in a manner that would honor her rather than simply expressing his own feelings. When God directed him to continue their relationship, he selflessly stayed with her at great cost to his personal reputation. His consistent obedience to God's instructions enabled him to pass the quality assurance checklist as a respectable leader. His life calls each of us to reflect for a moment to ask ourselves if we are leaders worthy of respect.

For further reflection and discussion:

1. Reflect on decisions you have made in the past week. Were they made based primarily on principle or feelings?

2. What results did they produce in my leadership and what can I learn from this?

3. What are the five most important guiding principles in my life?

   Are these consistently clear to those around me?

4. What have I done in my leadership in the past month to focus on the needs of others instead of my own desires?

5. To what extent do I model consistency with my life?

6. Am I focused on long-term gains or short-term wins?

7. Are there secret sins in my life that if exposed would diminish my influence? If so, what do I need to do about them?

44. QUALITY ASSURANCE: HOSPITABLE

The next instruction Paul gives young Timothy about the type of leaders who are worthy to be called servant leaders is *"hospitable"* (1 Timothy 3:2). To be hospitable is to be friendly and welcoming to strangers or guests. What in the world does what happens at home have to do with leadership? Paul recognizes that hospitality reveals at least three things in the heart of a leader, each of which is essential for servant leaders.

Hospitality displays a willingness to be transparent. Inviting someone to your home is a risky act of vulnerability! The moment you open your door to a guest and invite them into your home, they learn to know you on a much deeper level than they ever will in public. They will observe the way that you interact with your wife and children. They will notice what books and magazines you read. They will get a sense of your values as they interact with you at home. If you are not willing to be transparent, limit your leadership to the office or public arena! It's much easier to hide who you really are in public than at home.

Hospitality demonstrates a heart of service.
Hospitality is a lot of work! Even if it is only a simple meal, hospitality involves preparation, cleaning, washing dishes, and then focusing on the needs and desires of the visitors. If your visitors stay in your home overnight or for a longer period of time, hospitality may involve moving children around to make room for the visitors, preparing beds, changing your morning schedule, and cleaning after they leave. If you don't have the heart of a servant, don't bring people home! It's much easier to meet them in a restaurant or café and have a meal together.

Hospitality discloses a spirit of generosity.
Hospitality is costly. It will cost you the time that it takes to prepare, entertain, and serve. It will also cost money, likely spending more for food to prepare a special meal or at least sharing what you have. Generosity is not so much a matter of how much you possess but how much you are willing to release. Some of the most generous people I know have very little materially, but are rich in generosity, and they express it by sharing freely what they have. If you're not willing to share, don't invite people to your home! It's much easier to keep than to give.

A biblical example of a servant leader who demonstrated hospitality is the account of Simon, the Tanner. Luke records the story of how this worker in a despised vocation hosted the apostle Peter in his home for *"many days"* (Acts 9:43). We have no idea how many meals were served to Peter during this time, but we do know that he not only enjoyed the bedroom and the kitchen of Simon the Tanner, but he also had access to the roof where he went to pray. What is more, one day, three total strangers showed up and Peter, himself a guest, invited them in for the night! Another meal and three more beds! How would you respond to that kind of a guest? We know nothing else of Simon's faith, leadership, or academic credentials. But when he opened his door to Peter, God opened the door of faith to the Gentile world! Simon passed the quality checklist for a servant leader because of his hospitality. Peter was likely remembering him when he wrote later, *Offer hospitality to one another without grumbling* (1 Peter 4:9). How do you rate in this hidden area of leadership? Take some time to reflect on the questions below....and invite someone to your home today!

For further reflection and discussion:

1. When is the last time you invited someone to your home for a meal?   To spend the night?   Do you find hospitality easy or difficult?   Why?

2. What is the hardest for you in relation to hospitality: transparency, service, or generosity?

3. Spend a moment asking God to reveal to you what He wants to change in this area.

4. How does your culture encourage or discourage hospitality?

5. What can you do as a follower of Jesus to cultivate His culture in your home?

6. Reflect on Hebrews 13:2. How is God inviting you to respond in obedience?

45. QUALITY ASSURANCE: ABLE TO TEACH

Paul's quality checklist to Timothy next calls for leaders who are *"able to teach"* (1 Timothy 3:2). Many associate this skill with only a few select individuals who are gifted and called to public speaking and teaching. But Paul is convinced that all leaders should have this ability. He agrees with the writer of Hebrews who says to us all, *by this time you ought to be teachers* (Hebrews 5:12). Paul recognizes that being able to teach is for every servant leader because it reveals four key passions of their heart.

Able to teach reveals a love for learning. Effective teachers are passionate learners. They recognize that before they can teach others, they need to learn themselves. This learning can be formal or informal, but leaders who pass the quality assurance test *"able to teach"* are always learning and growing. They are eager to read, attend trainings, and learn from others who are ahead of them on the journey. They are willing to invest the time and resources required to learn. A love for learning requires thinking, reflecting, evaluating, and digesting information. Servant leaders love to learn not simply to impress others with their knowledge or credentials, but because they see themselves as stewards of the mind which God has given to them. They have a passion to learn as much as they can so that they glorify God by becoming all that God created them to be.

Able to teach reveals a love for others. Teachers are not simply passionate about personal growth but they desire to pass this on to others to see them also grow and develop. Leaders whose motives are selfish will learn and grow for their own benefit. But servant leaders' love for others motivates them to develop their teaching ability so they can help others grow. They recognize that their leadership is a sacred trust from God for the good of others and they deeply desire to see those under their leadership learning to grow as well.

Able to teach reveals a love for communication. Not all leaders will be skilled or gifted in the area of public communication. But all servant leaders have a passion to communicate well to others what God has taught them. A mother at home takes time over a cup of tea to communicate with a neighbor what she has learned about parenting. Corporate managers find emerging leaders and coach them to navigate the system. Pastors prepare to teach as a way of communicating with others what God has taught them through their study and experience. Servant leaders are passionate about communicating to others and continually seek to be more effective in this skill.

Able to teach reveals a love for transformation. Effective teachers recognize that the goal of teaching is not passing on information but life transformation. They take seriously the Great Commission's charge, *"teaching them to obey"* (Matthew 28:19). Servant leaders are passionate about producing change in the lives of those who follow and sharpen their teaching skills in an effort to see increasing transformation take place.

Ezra was a biblical leader who was well able to teach. A short description of his life provides a lot of insight for all servant leaders. *For Ezra had devoted himself to the study and observance of the Law of the LORD, and to teaching its decrees and laws in Israel* (Ezra 7:10). Note the progression: Ezra first studied, then obeyed, and then taught others. As his own life was transformed, he passed it on to others. He teaches all servant leaders not to teach without study which produces transformation. But he also challenges us after transformation to teach others. Take a moment to rate your leadership in the area of teaching.

For further reflection and discussion:

1. What am I doing to learn and grow this week?

   In the past month?

2. What books am I reading and what seminars have I attended?

3. Am I meeting with a mentor to help me grow? If not, who would be a good mentor for me?

4. Am I growing in wisdom, the ability to apply what I'm learning to life situations?

5. What is my attitude towards those whom I lead?

   Am I passionate about their growth?

6. Do I desire to see them develop their own skills and abilities?

7. Is my desire for their growth because of my love for them or is it simply because I want them to help me accomplish my vision?

8. How effective am I at communicating to others what God has taught?

   Am I growing in this area?

   Am I most effective in public or private settings?

9. What transformation do I see in the lives of those whom I am leading?

10. Are there ways that I can grow as a teacher which will result in greater transformation in their lives?

46. QUALITY ASSURANCE: NOT GIVEN TO DRUNKENNESS

Paul's list of qualifications next mentions that the leader is *"not given to drunkenness"* (1 Timothy 3:3). It seems obvious that Paul does not want to see leaders staggering after drinking too much alcohol. But his statement should cause even those who drink no alcohol to think more deeply about what he is saying. What is Paul's underlying concern and what does it have to do with servant leadership? Servant leaders recognize and avoid three distinct dangers of alcohol.

Servant leaders resist negative influences. We often describe a person drinking alcohol as "under the influence." The use of alcohol negatively influences the physical and mental capacity of the one who drinks. Judgment is impaired and often foolish decisions are made because of this influence. Servant leaders realize they are called to be influencers, and therefore carefully guard what influences them. They guard their relationships with persons who impact their attitudes and actions. They guard their eyes from images, movies, and pictures that will lead them in the wrong direction. Instead of being under the influence of alcohol, they seek to be increasingly under the influence of the Holy Spirit (Ephesians 5:18).

Servant leaders refuse to cover pain with addictions. Alcohol is an effective way to cover up pain, at least temporarily. Many people turn to drinking to wash away their sorrows. Alcohol quickly becomes an easy way to deal with disappointments, broken relationships, and deep feelings of inadequacy. The temporary relief reinforces the behavior and becomes an addiction. Many leaders attempt to cover pain, if not through alcohol, with other addictive behaviors. They may turn to pornography to deal with the pain of their own loneliness; they may become workaholics to cope with the pain of feeling insignificant. They may immerse themselves in sports, gambling, or hobbies that numb the pain in their souls. Servant leaders recognize that addictions are a cheap substitute for real healing and choose instead to expose their pain to the Spirit of God who provides genuine and lasting healing.

Servant leaders reject artificial transformation. Alcohol quickly changes a person's personality. Shy persons strike up conversations with strangers. Timid and insecure persons become loud and bold after a few drinks. Alcohol brings freedom from inhibitions and seemingly transforms those who are under the influence. These transformations, however, are counterfeit and temporary. No lasting change happens. In contrast, Paul desires for the Spirit of God to give us boldness and free us from the things that keep us down. Servant leaders recognize that genuine transformation is a product of the work of the Holy Spirit over time. They refuse to accept any artificial shortcuts.

King Xerxes is a biblical example of a leader who allowed alcohol to influence his decisions. In a drunken state he gave a foolish and arrogant command to his wife. When she refused to obey, he became angry and banished her from his presence. In the passion of the moment he felt like a man of power and would have made a good model for a contemporary beer commercial. Later, however, he regretted his foolish action (Read his story in Esther 1).

Take a moment to reflect on your own leadership. What influences are you allowing to shape you?

For further reflection and discussion:

1. What are the three key influences that shape my life?

2. What evidence has there been in my life in the past week that I am controlled by the Spirit?

3. What negative influences do I need to eliminate from my life?

4. Take a few minutes to ask the Holy Spirit to reveal any addictions in your life. Identify any behavior that is an attempt to deal with pain.

    In what way does God want to bring total healing to that area?

5. What areas of my life need transformation?

6. Am I cooperating with the Spirit to see this area changed or am I looking for shortcuts?

47. QUALITY ASSURANCE: NOT VIOLENT, BUT GENTLE

Paul next turns his attention to a heart issue of great importance to all leaders, *"not violent but gentle"* (1 Timothy 3:3). In that short phrase, Paul radically redefines what it means to lead. Most cultures honor military heroes, warriors who destroy all opposition by force, and we honor those who push their way to victory. Our national heroes ride gallant horses or fighter jets. They have power and use it violently to accomplish their objectives. Not many heroes are characterized by gentleness, but Paul calls each of us to lead, not with violence, but gentleness. What does it mean for us to lead in this way?

Gentle leaders surrender their own agenda. All leaders have a cause that gives them energy to move forward. Sadly, for most leaders, the cause is their own. They lead to accomplish their own agendas, and build their own kingdom. They are filled with desire to see their vision accomplished and use their power in any way possible to see it come to pass. No price is too great for their vision; they are determined to leave their mark on the world. Unfortunately, the mark has often been made with pain, division, blood, and tears as leaders violently pursue their selfish agenda. Christian leaders can quickly add a thin veneer of spirituality to their goals but at the root, it is about their desires, not God's. Paul calls leaders to surrender their own agenda, yielding their leadership to God's agenda and to replace a violent, aggressive spirit with gentleness. This requires a deep brokenness to the plan of God and recognition that all power comes from Him and is to be used for His purposes. There is no shortcut to this kind of brokenness as it demands a surrender of our own will to the Lordship of Jesus. Then, and only then, can a leader confidently, but gently, lead others to fulfill God's plans.

Gentle leaders influence from below. At first glance, it would seem that gentle leaders don't have a chance to make it in our competitive world. Jesus words, *"Blessed are the meek, for they will inherit the earth"* (Matthew 5:5) seem impossible for the 21st century. Leaders who exert power and use force seem to have more influence. But Paul recognizes that as servant leaders reject violence, they are in a position to influence from below. Their gentle spirits reflect a quiet strength of character that over time allows them to influence others in greater and more transformative ways than those who use their positions and power to influence others. Martin L. King, Mahatma Gandhi, and Nelson Mandela are recent examples of the way leaders can influence without positions and without violence.

Gentle leaders fight only for others. Servant leaders are not weak leaders, but they use their positions and influence to fight for others rather than themselves. They use their influence to fight for righteousness and justice. They champion the cause of the person with no voice and no influence. This is selfless leadership and gentle strength.

Moses is a biblical example of a gentle leader. In his youth he tried to accomplish God's plan through violence, but he later learned what it meant to lead with gentleness. He gently led through the rebellion of Korah, a test which would have caused many of us to use our power with force. He cried out to God for the sake of even those who opposed him and earned the title of the meekest man on the earth (See Numbers 12:3). Take a moment to reflect on what most characterizes your leadership: violence or gentleness.

For further reflection and discussion:

1. Is my leadership about myself or God? (Don't answer this too quickly!) Has there been a turning point in my leadership journey where I consciously surrendered my agenda to God's agenda?

2. Would others describe my leadership as pushy or gentle? In what ways has this been evident in my leadership in the past week?

3. When is the last time I used my influence to fight for someone without a voice?

48. QUALITY ASSURANCE: NOT QUARRELSOME

Paul continues to raise the standard for servant leaders and continues his quality assurance checklist by telling Timothy that a godly leader must not be *"quarrelsome"* (1 Timothy 3:3). "Quarrelsome" is a habitual inclination to disagree and stir up contention. The writer of Proverbs paints a colorful picture of a quarrelsome person, *As charcoal to embers and as wood to fire, so is a quarrelsome man for kindling strife* (Proverbs 26:21). Unfortunately, this describes the way some leaders use their influence. In contrast, servant leaders promote peace by demonstrating three of the fruits of the Spirit listed by Paul in Galatians 5:22-23.

Leaders who promote peace demonstrate love. Genuine love for others is expressed as leaders try to bring people together and resolve conflict. Leaders without love for others promote conflict. They use their words to incite conflict and bring division. As they do, they show only love for themselves and their own cause. They don't care about the wounds, death, and pain which will be inflicted on others as a result of their actions. Servant leaders care more about the welfare of those they lead than themselves. They desire the best for others because they love them. They genuinely want those they lead to be at peace with themselves and others and yield their own rights for the sake of those they love.

Leaders who promote peace demonstrate self-control. Many friendships have been broken by persons who could not control their tongue. On a larger scale, nations have been led into war by leaders who recklessly stir up hatred towards those of a different tribe, language or religion. They fan the flame of our natural sinful tendencies which also bring strife and division. Proverbs states, *Reckless words pierce like a sword, but the tongue of the wise brings healing* (Proverbs 12:18). Servant leaders learn to think carefully before speaking and to control their tongue. They control their own anger in an effort to promote peace.

Leaders who promote peace demonstrate patience. Promoting peace takes much patience. Selfish leaders want their opinion to be heard. They are more concerned about winning the argument than maintaining the relationship. They impatiently raise their voice and insist on being heard. Servant leaders patiently listen to the opinions of others and seek to find the common ground. They do not compromise truth but are not argumentative. They work patiently to bring people together. They do not give up after one failed attempt. Servant leaders recognize that promoting peace is often a long and difficult process and they are willing to pay the price.

A biblical example of a leader who deliberately avoided quarrels is Joseph, the Prime Minister of Egypt. He came from a contentious family with plenty of arguments and dissension. But he patiently and lovingly promoted peace. When in power, he could have used his authority to inflame wrongs from the past but he controlled himself for the good of others. As he sent his brothers home he gave them counsel which is just as valid for servant leaders today, *"Don't quarrel on the way!"* (Genesis 45:24). He did all that he could do to avoid quarrels.

For further reflection and discussion:

1. When is the last time you raised your voice in an argument? What does it indicate about the condition of your heart?

2. Would your family describe you as a peacemaker?

    What about those who work with you?

    Those under your leadership?

    What do you need to change?

3. Reflect on the following verses from Proverbs which talk about quarreling. Listen carefully to what God is speaking to your heart as you read them and write specific things you need to change. (Proverbs 15:18, 17:14, 17:19, 20:3, 26:17, 26:20).

49. QUALITY ASSURANCE: NOT A LOVER OF MONEY

As Paul continues to list what he expects from servant leaders, he turns next to the sensitive issue of money. A leader of quality will be *"not a lover of money"* (1 Timothy 3:3). Paul recognizes that loving money is a powerful temptation for all leaders. He later says to Timothy, *For the love of money is a root of all kinds of evil. Some people, eager for money, have wandered from the faith and pierced themselves with many griefs* (1Timothy 6:10). Paul's primary concern is not with the amount of money a leader has but with the heart attitude the leader has towards money. Servant leaders seek to honor God in the way they use money and clearly recognize the evil results of loving money.

Leaders who love money use people. Leaders who love money focus on how their leadership can increase their personal income or help them to achieve their own financial goals. Whether the followers are workers in a business or members of a congregation, the leader looks at them as a way to prosper. They are producers of income and sources of finance. They see the people they lead as means towards their selfish ends. However, servant leaders see the people they lead as gifts from God and honor them by investing in their lives to see them develop. They focus on developing others rather than using them for their own benefit.

Leaders who love money compromise integrity. Leaders who love money will inevitably begin to make decisions based primarily on what will be most profitable. They will begin to take shortcuts, engage in questionable business practices, develop friendships based on what the other person has to offer financially, etc. These actions can easily be justified as normal since so many others are also doing the same. However, servant leaders refuse to compromise their integrity for financial gain. They make some decisions that will provide less income simply because the decision is right. They treat the poor with the same respect as those with much.

Leaders who love money reject God. This statement may seem overly judgmental; however, Jesus makes it clear that between God and money, only one will be the master (Matthew 6:24). When leaders choose to build their leadership around money or profit, they have unconsciously rejected God's rule and authority over their lives. Money becomes an idol that controls how they lead, the decisions they make, and the way they relate to others. Servant leaders recognize this sobering reality and consciously seek first God's Kingdom, not material gain. They learn to be content with what they have, view themselves as stewards of all that God has given to them, and surrender their finances to the Lordship of Jesus. They give generously, and as they do are set free from the tyranny of loving money.

The sad story of Ananias and Sapphira (Acts 5:1-10) serves as a biblical example of the danger of loving money. Ironically, in the midst of an act of giving, this couple was guilty of loving money. Outwardly they looked good, but they desired to use money to gain favor and respect from others. They compromised truth in their report to Peter and tragically lost their lives as a result. Their sudden death should cause each of us to pause and ask ourselves if there are ways that our own hearts reflect a love of money.

For further reflection and discussion:

1. Are any of the following warning signs of loving money in my life and leadership? If so, what corrective steps should I take?

   I see the people I lead as sources of money for myself.

   I treat people differently based on the amount of money they have.

   I make decisions based on potential loss or profit more than whether it is right or wrong.

   I find it difficult to give sacrificially.

   I do not experience genuine contentment with what I have.

2. Reflect on the following scriptures. (Matthew 6:24; Luke 12:15; 16:13-14; Hebrews 13:5, Philippians 4:12; 1 Timothy 6:9-10) What is the Lord speaking to your heart through them?

50. QUALITY ASSURANCE: MANAGES FAMILY WELL

Paul has already listed 11 challenging items for Timothy to consider when looking at the quality of leaders. He is near to the end of his list and shifts his attention to something obviously close to his heart. *He must manage his own family well and see that his children obey him with proper respect. (If anyone does not know how to manage his own family, how can he take care of God's church?)* (1 Timothy 3:4-5). Paul feels so strongly about the leader's family life that he doesn't just list the quality but provides an explanation of why it is so critical. Servant leaders recognize that their leadership in the public sphere is connected to their leadership at home.

The leader's family is preparation for other leadership. Paul recognizes that servant leadership is homegrown. It happens first in the close, daily relationships of family life. Both men and women learn to lead by first influencing those who are closest to them. Leading in the family prepares a leader to lead others. We learn what sacrificial and unconditional love is as we share life together in our homes. Parenting children allows us to develop the Father heart of God towards others. At home we are all most likely to allow sinful expressions of selfishness and pride to emerge. Servant leaders allow God to use these experiences to prepare them to lead others.

The leader's family is a predictor of other leadership. Paul implies that the way a leader functions at home is the best indicator of how he or she will function in other leadership roles. His simple statement offers an alternative to expensive personality tests designed to determine if someone will succeed as a leader. Paul's principle is that if a leader rules with an iron hand at home, it is likely that the same will be true at the office. If a leader learns to serve and deny self at home, it will come naturally in other leadership roles. If a leader puts career ahead of family, he will call others to likewise give their best to an organization instead of family. Servant leaders are first identified at home.

Family leadership is a prerequisite for other leadership. Paul speaks to church leaders and notes that if a leader cannot manage his own family, he cannot care for people at church. Faithful leadership at home is a requirement for successful leadership at work, in the community, at church, or in a business. Tragically, many of us pay more attention to developing our leadership at work than at home. We measure our leadership success by how quickly we move up organizational ladders. Paul calls us to reexamine our priorities. Servant leaders make their leadership at home a priority.

Paul's standard may seem unrealistically high and too narrow for modern society. Paul's strong words about our families do not imply that if a child rebels we are quickly disqualified for leadership. But his concern about our leadership at home should cause each of us to pause and take a closer look at what is happening in our leadership at home.

The Bible is filled with examples of leaders who succeeded and failed at home. David is perhaps the clearest example of a leader who seemed to succeed at every endeavor except at home. He passionately loved and worshipped God and lead with a great heart and excellent leadership skills (Psalm 78:72). But his poor leadership at home tarnished his otherwise great record. His own moral failures began with Bathsheba and he lost one child through that tragedy. He allowed the rape of his daughter to go unchecked and as a result reaped the rebellion and death of his son Absalom, and the near loss of the kingdom. He reminds all of us that the true test of our leadership is not on the job but at home.

Take a moment to reflect on the way you lead at home by answering the questions below.

For further reflection and discussion:

1. In what ways has your leadership at home shaped the way you lead others?

2. What leadership lessons have been most significant for you to learn at home?

3. How would my family describe my leadership? Would they use words like loving, compassionate, and strong or words like harsh, judgmental, and self-serving?

4. Think of a recent, difficult situation at home. How did you lead your family through this situation? Did you express servant leadership or selfish leadership in this situation?

5. What have you done recently to strengthen your leadership at home? Are you reading books, attending seminars, or talking with a mentor to improve your leadership at home?

51. QUALITY ASSURANCE: NOT A NEW CONVERT

Paul continues his quality checklist for Timothy by noting that the leaders chosen must *not be a recent convert, or he may become conceited and fall under the same judgment as the devil* (1 Timothy 3:6). At first glance it may seem like Paul is against young leaders. However, he is writing these words to Timothy, a young leader. Timothy, although young, had been a believer in Christ for many years and was not a recent convert. Paul's instruction is not focused on age but maturity in faith. Paul's instruction implies that even if a seasoned leader comes to faith in Christ, time is needed before he or she is ready to be a servant leader. Paul recognizes leadership maturity does not automatically develop with time but cannot develop without it. Time provides experience that allows leaders to mature and develop. There are no shortcuts or ways to speed up the process. The only thing which can be done is to effectively use the time to produce maximum maturity. Servant leaders do this in several ways.

Servant leaders use time to reflect on their experiences. Leaders automatically gain experience with time; the question is what they do with that experience. Servant leaders learn the discipline of reflection to turn their experiences into wisdom. They use time for reflection to learn from their mistakes as well as successes. As they reflect, they are able to identify personal deficiencies in character and ask God to change them. They identify weaknesses in competence and develop plans to strengthen their skill. In reflection, they learn to hear God's quiet voice giving direction. They take time to reflect because they desire to maximize their experience for the glory of God. Inexperienced leaders often impulsively keep running ahead with little time to stop and reflect.

Servant leaders use time to gain new experiences. Servant leaders acknowledge that time is a precious gift from God to enable them to carry out the vision that He has given to them. They see each day as an opportunity to grow and gain new experience that will allow them to more completely fulfill that vision. They recognize that God's plan for growth demands that they continually stretch their own capacity to lead. They refuse to be satisfied in their comfort zone. They recognize that if they are not growing in gaining new experience in leadership, a much younger leader will soon surpass their maturity. Inexperienced leaders quickly stop growing and stretching.

Servant leaders use time to share their experiences. Servant leaders are not simply interested in building their own personal leadership potential; their focus is on serving others. They want to build into the next generation what God has taught them and actively find ways to do this. This happens sometimes informally; at other times in public speaking events, or through deliberate writing or blogging about their experience. Inexperienced leaders overlook opportunities to invest in the next generation.

Paul himself is a great example of a servant leader who was not a recent convert. He took 3 years in the desert before any act of leadership. He continually reflected on his leadership and acknowledged *I have not yet obtained all this.* He continually yearned for more with a vision for the "regions beyond." He continually invested his life and experience into younger leaders, including this passage he wrote to Timothy (See Galatians 1:18; Philippians 3:12; 2 Corinthians 10:16; and 2 Timothy 2:2). He used time to build leadership maturity.

Take a moment to ask yourself if your leadership maturity equals the time you have followed Jesus.

For further reflection and discussion:

1. Do you build into your schedule time for reflection?

    If not, what needs to change?

    If so, what have you been learning about yourself and leadership in the past 3 months?

2. Reflect on a mistake that you have made in leadership. What did you learn from that experience?

    Have you made changes in your leadership to avoid repeating that mistake?

3. What new leadership challenges have you faced in the last 6 months and how have you responded to them?

    Have you used them as opportunities to grow and develop your leadership ability?

4. Are there leadership opportunities before you which you have not accepted simply because you know they will require greater levels of

commitment and sacrifice?

If so, what will it take for you to move out of your comfort zone?

5. Have you deliberately invested in the life of a younger leader, freely sharing your experience with them?

If not, what is God inviting you to do in this area?

6. Are there opportunities God has given to you to share your experience with others that you have declined? (This could be opportunities to speak or share with the group publicly, an opportunity to write or teach either formally or informally.)

If so, reflect on why you missed this opportunity and what needs to change.

7. If you are a young leader, what are you doing to deliberately learn from those who have more experience than you?

52. QUALITY ASSURANCE: GOOD REPUTATION WITH OUTSIDERS

Paul ends his list of qualifications for servant leaders as he tells Timothy, *He must also have a good reputation with outsiders, so that he will not fall into disgrace and into the devil's trap* (1 Timothy 3:7). Paul's instruction implies that the true test of our leadership capacity is not with those who agree with us, but those who are "outsiders" or those who do not agree with our faith. This does not make popularity a condition of servant leadership. Nor does this imply that no one will criticize or reject our positions, especially when we take a stand on unpopular issues. Paul himself faced intense opposition. But it means that in every way possible, servant leaders live in ways that build good reputations with those who do not share their views and faith. They build good reputations in several ways.

A servant leader builds a good reputation with integrity. Servant leaders refuse to compromise God's standards in how they use their money, their power, or their relationships. This integrity, in a world where bribery, lies, and unfaithfulness are common, makes the life of the servant leader shine like a bright light in the darkness. They model 1 Peter 2:12, *Live such good lives among the pagans that, though they accuse you of doing wrong, they may see your good deeds and glorify God on the day he visits us.* Outsiders may respond with jeers or with vicious attacks, but they recognize that the servant leader is blameless.

A servant leader builds a good reputation with consistency. A good reputation is built only with time. Servant leaders keep doing what they are supposed to do day after day, week after week, and year after year. They are not concerned with short-term gains, but focus on long-term consistency.

A servant leader builds a good reputation with love. The real test for servant leaders is not only in their actions in relationship to outsiders, but in their heart attitude towards them. Leaders naturally hold strong opinions and have learned how to effectively communicate them to others. But a leader's heart is revealed when relating to persons who disagree. It is easy to see those who disagree with us as the enemy, as wrong, as somehow less valuable. But servant leaders view these "outsiders" with love. They are as concerned about the relationship as they are about being right. They show restraint even when provoked by false accusations or slander. They seek opportunities to talk face-to-face. They recognize that *love covers a multitude of sins* (1 Peter 4:8).

Integrity, consistently practiced in a spirit of love, builds a good reputation even with "outsiders." In doing so, servant leaders guard against falling into disgrace and the 'devil's trap' which can quickly undermine the leaders' ability to influence for good.

Timothy himself serves as a biblical example of a leader who had a good reputation with others. Before

Paul selected him to be a member of his team, Luke records that *the brothers at Lystra and Iconium spoke well of him* (Acts 16:2). Timothy's own father was an unbeliever but allowed Timothy to join this missionary team which continually represented Christ in places where the church did not exist.

With this, Paul's list is complete. He sets a high standard for those who lead as followers of Jesus. While none of us perfectly measure up to the standard, let's resist the temptation to lower the standard. Rather, join me in asking Jesus to make us leaders of the highest quality as we represent Him in our place of influence.

For further reflection and discussion:

1. Who are the 'outsiders' in my life and leadership?

    In what ways has God given me opportunities to influence them?

    What kind of reputation do I currently have with them?

2. On a scale of 1 to 10, how consistently have I represented Jesus to these "outsiders"?

3. When people disagree with my position or view, what is the attitude of my heart towards them?

    How is that attitude expressed?

4. Go to someone you consider an "outsider" who you know has significantly different opinions than you. Ask them to share with you how you come across to them. As appropriate, ask their forgiveness and share your desire to show them respect and love.

EPILOGUE

I hope you've enjoyed the journey; I have certainly enjoyed walking with you through these pages as we consider the options to be selfish or servant leaders. It's not easy to make the right choices, but I hope you agree with me that the rewards of servant leadership are far greater than the costs. What a privilege it is to learn from those who have gone before us and to imitate the example of Jesus. I suspect He's far more involved in our journeys than we can imagine, and I'm sure He has much more ahead! Keep leading like Him and doing your part to impact our world. Move on to volume 2 in this series.

Yours on the journey,
Jon Byler

ABOUT THE AUTHOR

Jon Byler has a passion to see church leaders grow and develop into mature, Christ-like leaders. He is committed to developing a worldwide alliance of leadership training programs through his role as the Director of LEAD, a part of the Global Disciples Alliance. He lived in Thika, Kenya for 13 years and currently resides in Lancaster, Pennsylvania, USA. He and his wife Loice are the parents of three children. He has experience as a pastor, has authored several books, and writes a bi-weekly e-zine, "Reflections for Servant Leaders."

(Subscribe on his website www.LeadersServe.com)

The Heart of Christian Leadership
The Art of Christian Leadership
7 Keys to Financial Freedom
Preaching to Change Lives, a homiletics textbook
Use that Gift, a study of spiritual gifts
Pits, Prisons and Palaces, a study of the life of Joseph
Steps to Maturity, a 10-lesson discipleship course
Free at Last, a study of deliverance
The Christian and Authority
A Church With a Purpose, A Bible Study Guide Series based on Rick Warren's *Five Purposes for a Church.*

ABOUT GLOBAL DISCIPLES

Global Disciples empowers clusters of churches to equip their people to share the Good News of Jesus with least-reached people, often in restricted areas. We partner with the local or indigenous church – committed believers who are motivated, focused, and effective communicators, and familiar with the language, culture, and customs. We provide a training model which can be used to train and send out fellow believers as mission workers to multiply Christ-like disciples and plant locally-sustained churches among least-reached people.

As Global Disciples:

- Our **Vision** is to see **every person** have an opportunity to **choose and follow Jesus Christ.**
- Our **Prayer** is that **disciples of Jesus Christ** from all nations and many vocations, will embrace this vision and **do their part.**
- Our **Mission** is to make it possible for **clusters of churches** to multiply Christ-like disciples and locally-sustainable fellowships in **least-reached areas.**
- Our **Philosophy** is that local expressions of the Body of Christ **in close proximity** to least-reached peoples are best able to reach them – and **we all can help.**

About Global Disciples Alliance

Global Disciples Alliance is an association of transformational trainings that are Christ-centered, discipleship-based and mission-focused. Training programs in the Alliance share this vision to multiply transformational trainings in the areas of discipleship/mission, leadership development, and small business development for church planters.

For more information about Global Disciples, LEAD, or Global Disciples Alliance, please visit our website at www.GlobalDisciples.org, or contact us below.

Global Disciples
315 W James St., Suite 202
Lancaster, PA. 17603

OTHER BOOKS BY JON BYLER

All are available in print and electronic form on
www.Amazon.com

The Heart of Christian Leadership
This book focuses on character issues for
servant leaders. It is filled with practical
examples of how to develop the heart of
Jesus in leadership. Assignments for each
chapter make it ideal for individual or
group use.

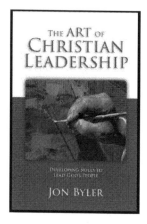

The Art of Christian Leadership
This book deals with skill issues in
leadership and is a practical guide
for developing leadership skills
needed by all leaders.

7 Keys to Financial Freedom
Discover Biblical truth about finances
that will set you free! Bible Study
guide is included.

Made in the USA
Middletown, DE
23 November 2018